# stitch magic

# stitch magic

## sculpting fabric with stitch

alison j. reid

A & C BLACK • LONDON

*To Mum and Dad, Pam and Clive*

**Stitch Magic**
First published in 2011 by
A & C Black Publishers
36 Soho Square
London W1D 3QY
www.acblack.com



Created and produced by Berry & Bridges Ltd
Suite 416, Belsize Business Centre
258 Belsize Road
London NW6 4BT

**Designer** Anne Wilson
**Editor** Katie Hardwicke
**Photography (projects and fabrics)** John Heseltine
**Photography (design samples)** Ed Berry
**Line illustrations** Alison J. Reid
**Stylist** Susan Berry

British Library of Congress Publication Data
A catalogue record of this book is available from the British Library

ISBN 978-1-4081-2262-4

Reproduced and printed in Singapore

# contents

# introduction

I have been sewing for many years and never fail to be excited by the myriad effects that can be achieved by combining different fabrics with different stitches. With a little bit of imagination and only a little skill you can create unusual and exciting fabrics of your own. This book is about the magic of that process. Serendipity often offers the most unexpected results, so never be afraid to experiment. When you have purchased a new piece of fabric, play with it for a while before you decide what to make with it. What happens when it's folded? Does it crease? Does it fray when cut? What happens when you layer it with another fabric? You need to be sensitive to its properties to get the best from it, and the answers to these questions, plus plenty more besides, play an important role in determining the success you have in manipulating and stitching fabric.

I find my own inspiration from a variety of different sources: it could be from watching a film, seeing a garment in a shop window display or studying a flower in my back garden. I like to keep a sketchbook and small digital camera with me all the time so I can make records of what inspires me, and store them for future use. It's so easy to make a little sketch with a few notes or to take a photograph to record colour. A sketchbook is an invaluable resource for every would-be designer, as something you recorded weeks ago can easily be retrieved in the future to inform your latest design decisions.

Each chapter in this book is dedicated to a different technique for creating unique fabrics, ranging from cutting and folding shapes to pleating and cording in new ways. I have used a variety of different fabrics, everything from heavy Melton wools to fine cotton voiles. I have also injected colour and pattern here and there by using printed cotton fabric. In the design samples, I have experimented with different fabrics and threads to provide a gallery of inspirational ideas, which I hope will stir your creativity and encourage you to begin to manipulate and stitch fabrics in your own way to develop your own individual style.

Each chapter concludes with a couple of projects, some very easy, some a little more complicated. I have written the instructions using the techniques I find easiest, but you don't need to follow them slavishly. Once you have the general gist, you can experiment with your own methods and ideas. For each of my projects, I have chosen a fabric design inspired by the design samples in that chapter. You don't have to choose the design sample I did – it's up to you to work out what suits you best.

Hopefully, this book will give you the confidence to find your own style and, in the process, you will have lots of fun. Don't be afraid to make mistakes, sometimes mistakes lead to new inspiration and ideas for the future. Keep a record of whatever you create, and enjoy the magic!

# fabrics and threads

I prefer to use natural fabrics whenever possible. They are generally much easier to work with than synthetics and feel more pleasing in the hand. They also tend to wash and wear well, if treated with care.

My colour palette is fairly limited, and where I do use colour, it is often as an accent on an otherwise plain design. However, I do love beautiful prints too, using pattern again as a highlight or to accent part of the design. In general, the small-patterned printed cottons tend to work best with the style of designs I prefer, and I am a great fan of retro-style, little repeating patterns in mid-tones. Searching through charity shops and markets often results in some great fabric finds and I regularly buy old garments that I can cut up for the fabric alone.

**Fabric types and weights**

**Cotton** Lots of different weights of cottons have been used for the samples and projects in this book. They range from heavy-duty cottons, like denim or sailcloth, to lightweight diaphanous organdies and voiles. Explore what is available as the different weights will produce markedly different results. The smooth, flat cottons take dye very well and are often used for some exquisite prints, while the very fine cottons have a translucent quality about them. All cottons wash and wear well, do not fray much and are easy to sew.

**Linen** This is one of the world's oldest textiles and is used for both upholstery and garments. It is notorious for creasing, so linen mixes have been created, such as a cotton and linen blend, to prevent this. Linen is expensive but vintage shops are a treasure trove for antique bed linens that can be transformed into new textile pieces. Linen also washes and wears very well, and is easy to stitch.

**Silk** This is a luxurious fabric, available in light as well as heavier weights. Silk can be either matte or have a sheen to the surface, and the lightest weight silks, like silk organza, are translucent. Silk's lustre is distinctive, and silk handles and drapes well. Fine silks need to be stitched with the appropriate weight needle to ensure the fabric threads do not pull. Heavier weight silks are easier to sew and if pressed well can have a crisp, sharp look about them. Silk can be hand-washed with care at low temperatures.

**Wool** This has a naturally resilient spring in the fibres, which means it drapes well. There are many different qualities of wool, from the finest cashmeres and alpacas to more everyday wools and wool blends, and the yarns can be spun and plied to produce different weights. The fibres can also be felted to provide an extremely versatile fabric that can be cut with very little or no fraying at all. Wools are generally easy to stitch. They are sometimes mixed with other natural fibres or with small quantities of synthetics or microfibres to improve washability. Pure wools need to be hand-washed with care.

**Sewing threads and yarns**

For many of the samples and projects in this book, I have used ordinary sewing cotton. With natural fabrics, it is best to use pure cotton thread. Six-stranded embroidery threads are good where the stitching requires more emphasis. Wool yarns break easily and are only successful for decorative stitching. Use a suitable needle for the thickness of the chosen thread.

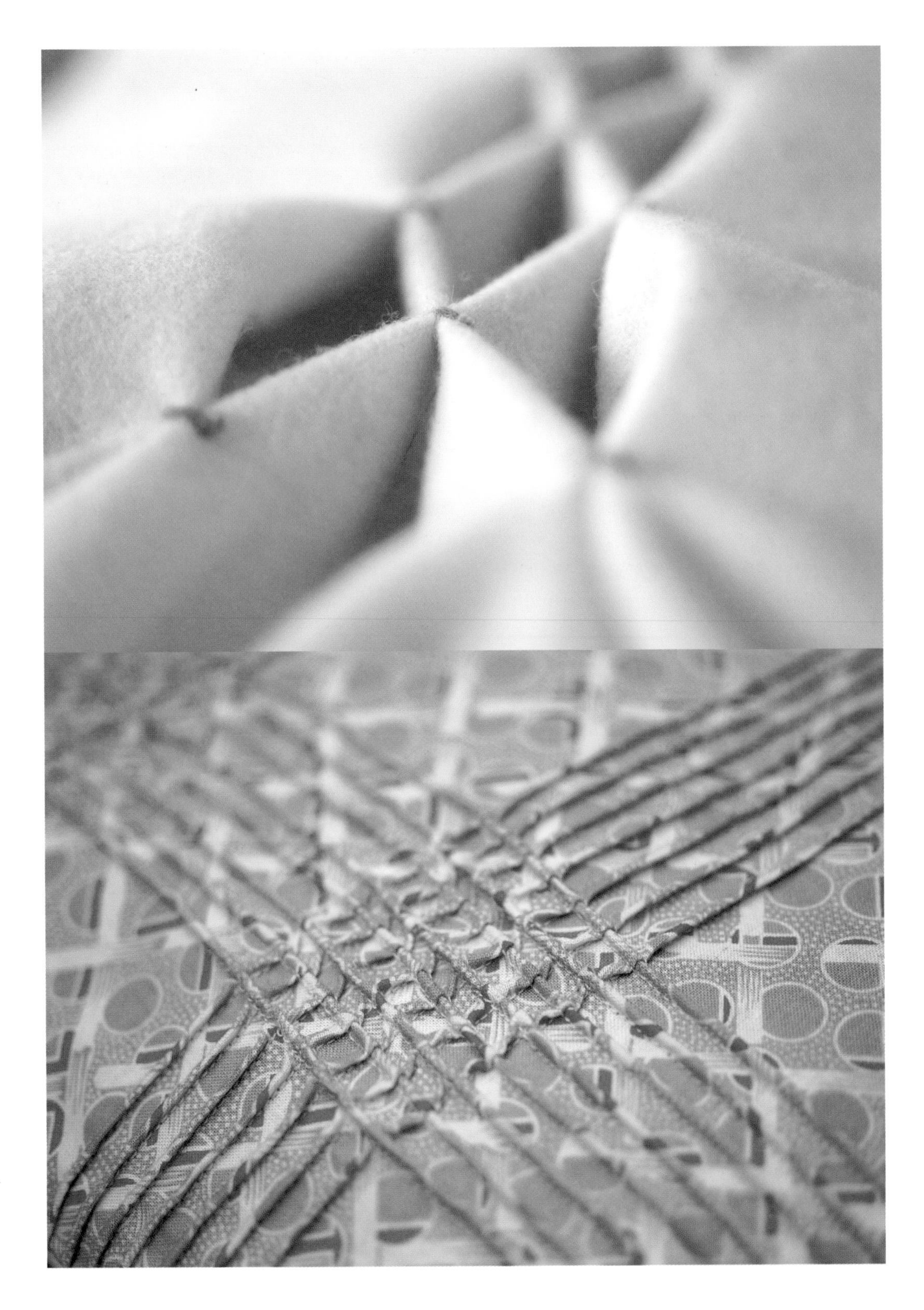

# getting started

There are a few things to consider before you begin to sew. If you follow these simple guidelines then your work will look more professional. Before you start working, set up an ironing board and iron, and a large table to cut out fabric. Ideally, you should also have a pinboard where you can pin up samples of your designs. Keep a notebook handy for recording information. Organize your basic equipment (see below) and keep it in a sewing box.

You may also need other specialist items, such as rotary cutters or a revolving hole punch. These will be listed at the start of each project.

**Before you start**

▶ Always press your fabric to remove any creases before you begin to cut it out.

▶ Choose the correct scissors for the job and make sure they are sharp. Use embroidery scissors for snipping off the threads and working with more intricate areas of cutting out. Use larger, heavier blades for cutting out large pattern pieces. A rotary cutter is good for cutting out long strips of fabric.

▶ Before cutting fabric, check that you are working on the straight grain of the weave. The straight grain is the line of threads running parallel to the selvedge (known as the warp). When important, the straight grain is marked as a horizontal or vertical arrow on the illustrated pattern piece. The bias of a fabric is indicated by an arrow running at a 45-degree angle to the straight grain. The weft of the fabric refers to the threads running horizontal to the selvedge.

▶ Take careful measurements before you cut your fabric and ensure you transfer any essential marked positions before you cut or sew.

▶ When cutting out, remember to allow enough fabric for seam allowances. They should generally be 1.5cm (½in) unless otherwise stated.

▶ Use a set square and ruler when cutting fabric with squared-up edges. To cut fabric straight, match the edge of a set square to the selvedge and mark the cutting line with a fabric-marking pencil.

▶ To find the centre of a piece of fabric, fold over and match up the straight edges. This can be done both horizontally and vertically. Use a dressmaking pin to mark the central point.

▶ Use paper or newsprint to sample a new pattern or design. Making a paper mock-up version prior to using your chosen fabric could save you money and prevent expensive mistakes.

### ● ● ● BASIC SEWING KIT

- fabric-marking pencils or tailor's chalk
- scissors in varying sizes: dressmaking shears, pinking shears and small embroidery scissors
- measuring equipment: tape, ruler, compass and set square
- hand-sewing needles in various sizes
- dressmaking pins
- standard sewing machine thread in various colours
- embroidery threads

**As you work**

▶ Where your pattern has a number of cut pieces, keep them in neat piles or containers, so that you can access them easily as you work.

▶ When sewing seams, press the folded seams in position and then pin or tack. When the seams are complete, press them open so that they lie flat and do not give an awkward bulkiness to your project. Clip curved seam allowances to help them lie flat. Clip seam allowances at corners for the same reason.

▶ When hemming fabric, fold the fabric over once by 5mm (¼in), press in position, fold again by the same amount, press and pin or tack. Then hand or machine stitch as required.

### ● ● ● SPECIAL SEWING KIT

- pre-formed templates
- revolving hole punch
- Stitch 'n' Tear stabilizer fabric
- dissolvable fabric (Aquafilm)
- smocking transfer grid paper
- wadding for quilting
- embroidery hoop
- special feet for sewing machine, such as quilting, pintucking, cording feet
- rotary cutter

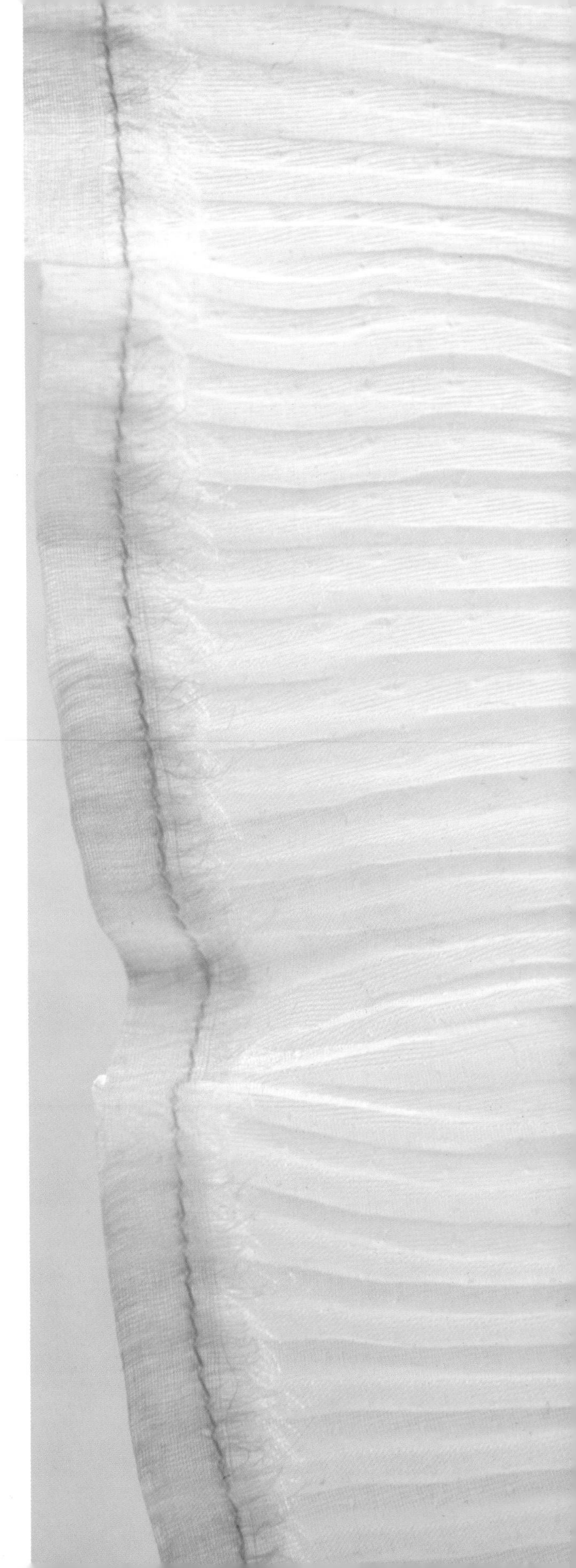

# cut shapes

There are many different ways to cut shapes to apply to a base fabric. Your choice of cutting tool will help to ensure a professional finish, so make sure you choose the right one for your chosen fabric and shape. Rotary cutters are great for cutting lengths of fabric into long strips; dressmaking shears allow you to cut large shapes with ease; and small embroidery scissors offer the best control when cutting more intricate little shapes. Professional textile designers also have access to specialist dye-cutting tools that cut out specific shapes very quickly. Laser cutting is now used extensively in the textile industry: in this process the design is digitized using computer software, then downloaded to a specialist laser cutting machine that cuts the fabric in the chosen pattern.

The style and size of your chosen design will determine your choice of fabric weights – from heavy-duty felt to the lightest of silks. You can incorporate the ways that different fabrics react when cut into your designs. For example, Melton wool does not fray, denim barely frays and fine silk frays very easily. These different attributes will affect the final look of your project.

I created the design samples in this chapter by cutting shapes in different sizes, shapes and fabrics and stitching them to various plain and patterned base fabrics. My preference is to keep the colour palette limited and the cut shapes uncomplicated. Experiment and see what you like.

◀ This monochrome, sculptural fabric is created from glazed linen circles applied to a felted wool base, stitched in neat, overlapping rows. The belt and mat on pages 18 and 22 are made using this fabric design.

# ● design samples

There are many different ways to create fabrics from cut and stitched shapes, using just one or two fabrics for the cut shapes and another for the base fabric. The design samples shown here are just a few possibilities from the myriad combinations of cut shapes, fabrics, colours and patterns that could be employed. Each uses a very similar technique (see pages 16–17) in which hand-cut shapes are machine or hand stitched in rows to a backing fabric. A limited colour palette and small repeating cut shapes – circles, rectangles and triangles – give the most graphic effects. At their very simplest (like the black circles shown on the belt on page 18) these cut-shape designs have a strong sculptural quality. Layering one shape on top of another or using a patterned fabric for the base, in a harmonious or contrasting colour, offers yet more design possibilities.

When trying out your own designs, make up several slightly different samples and pin them to a board in your workspace. Looking at them both close-up and from a distance changes the way you perceive them – worth considering when creating textile projects to complement existing interior design schemes or items in your wardrobe.

For the cut circles in the design samples here a special pre-formed circle template was used, available in art supply stores. When you draw your chosen circle size using the template, work on the wrong side of the fabric with a drawing pencil. For the rectangles or squares, make a card template using a ruler and then use this to cut the fabric shapes.

A

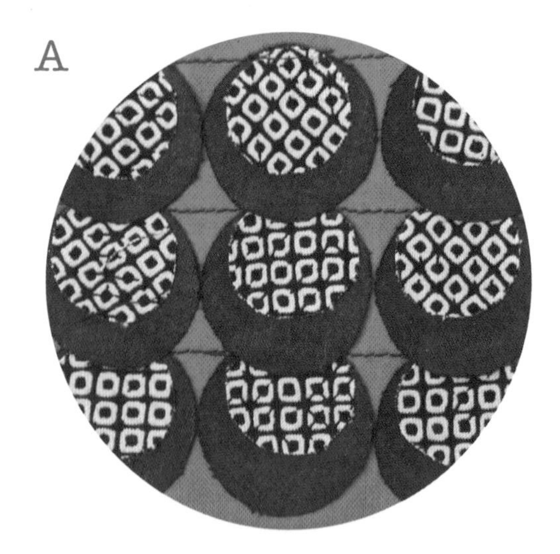

▲ **Sample A:** Two different-sized circles, one in plain, one in patterned fabric, are placed on top of each other. The rows of circles are machine stitched in neat lines across the contrasting base fabric, over the top edge of the circles.

B

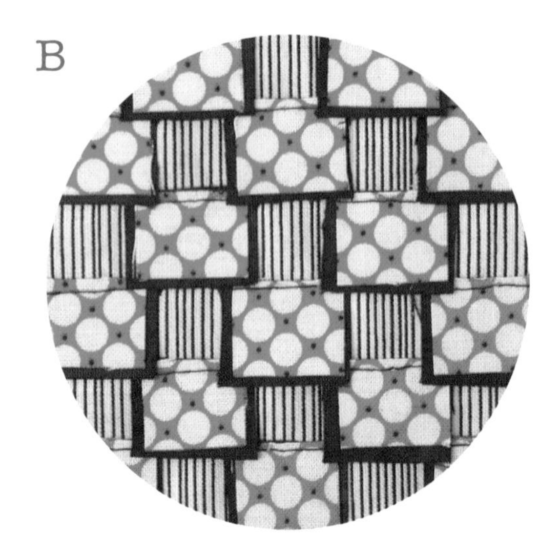

▲ **Sample B:** This sample is a similar construction to Sample A but here two sizes of rectangle are placed on top of each other. Like the circles in Sample A , the rows and columns overlap and are machine stitched to the striped base fabric across the top in neat rows.

C

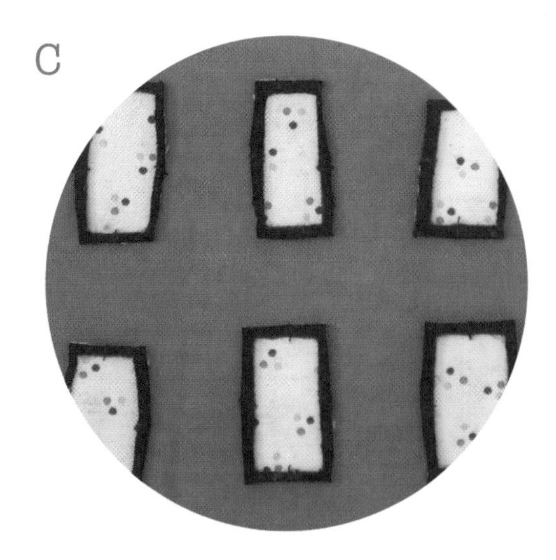

▲ **Sample C:** Two rectangles of a plain fabric and a patterned fabric are applied to a backing fabric. The plain black fabric has been cut away with small embroidery scissors to show the patterned fabric beneath. The rectangles are hand stitched to the base fabric.

E

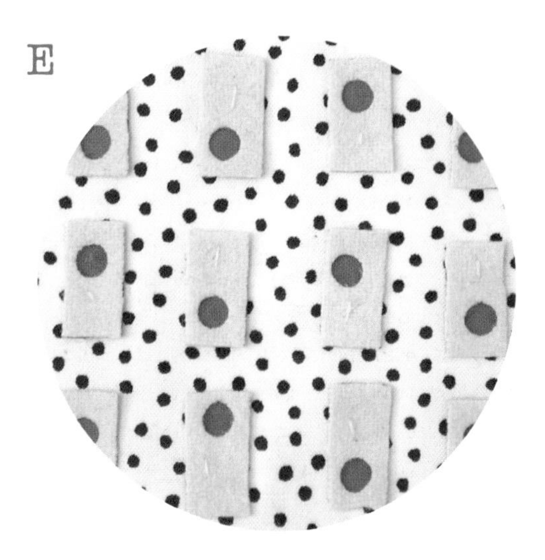

▲ **Sample E:** This is a similar construction to Sample C, but here a revolving hole punch has been used to cut little holes in the cream fabric, to reveal the red fabric beneath. Again, the rectangles are hand stitched to the spotted base fabric.

D

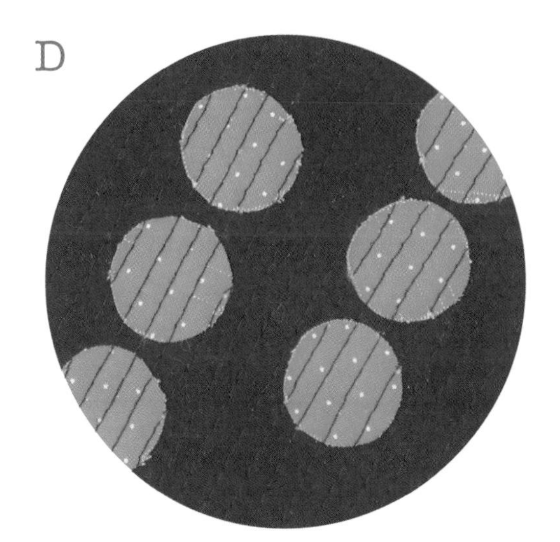

▲ **Sample D:** This is a variation of Sample A, using only one fabric for the cut shapes, randomly spaced and machine stitched in diagonal rows to the backing fabric. Using a thread that matches the backing fabric creates an additional design feature.

F

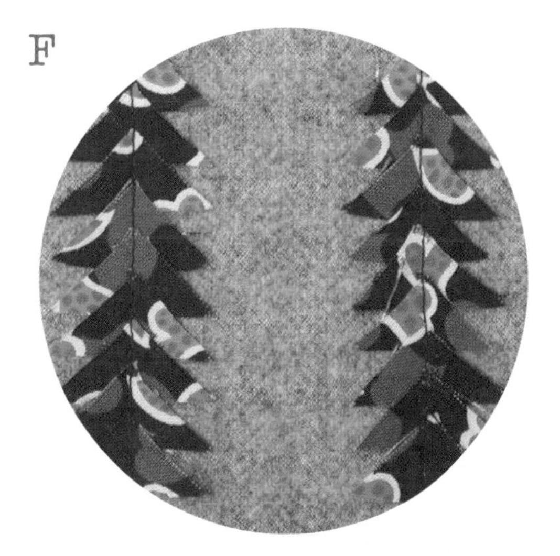

▲ **Sample F:** Small triangles of printed fabric have been created by cutting squares diagonally in half. The triangles are placed in overlapping rows on a plain base fabric, then machine stitched down the centre of each row.

# how to cut and stitch shapes

First, decide which fabric or fabrics you want to use for your design and the shapes you want to create. To estimate the quantity of fabric for a specific project it is a good idea to begin by making a small paper sample of your chosen shape, such as the rectangle in Sample B, and use this to multiply up the quantities of fabric required.

**Cutting out the shapes**

Always press your fabric before cutting to eliminate any creases. If you are using a patterned fabric, make sure that the template you use to cut the shapes lies on the straight grain (see page 10). The best cutting tool for the job will depend on the size and style of the cut shape. For large shapes and long strips, large scissors (**1**) or a rotary cutter (**2**) are best. For more intricate shapes, like the ones used in this chapter, you will find small, sharp embroidery scissors are ideal (**3**).

You can also experiment with the edges of the shapes. Why not cut them out using pinking shears (**4**)? These special dressmaking scissors are used to create a jagged edge that prevents fabric fraying, so they have a practical purpose too. Alternatively,

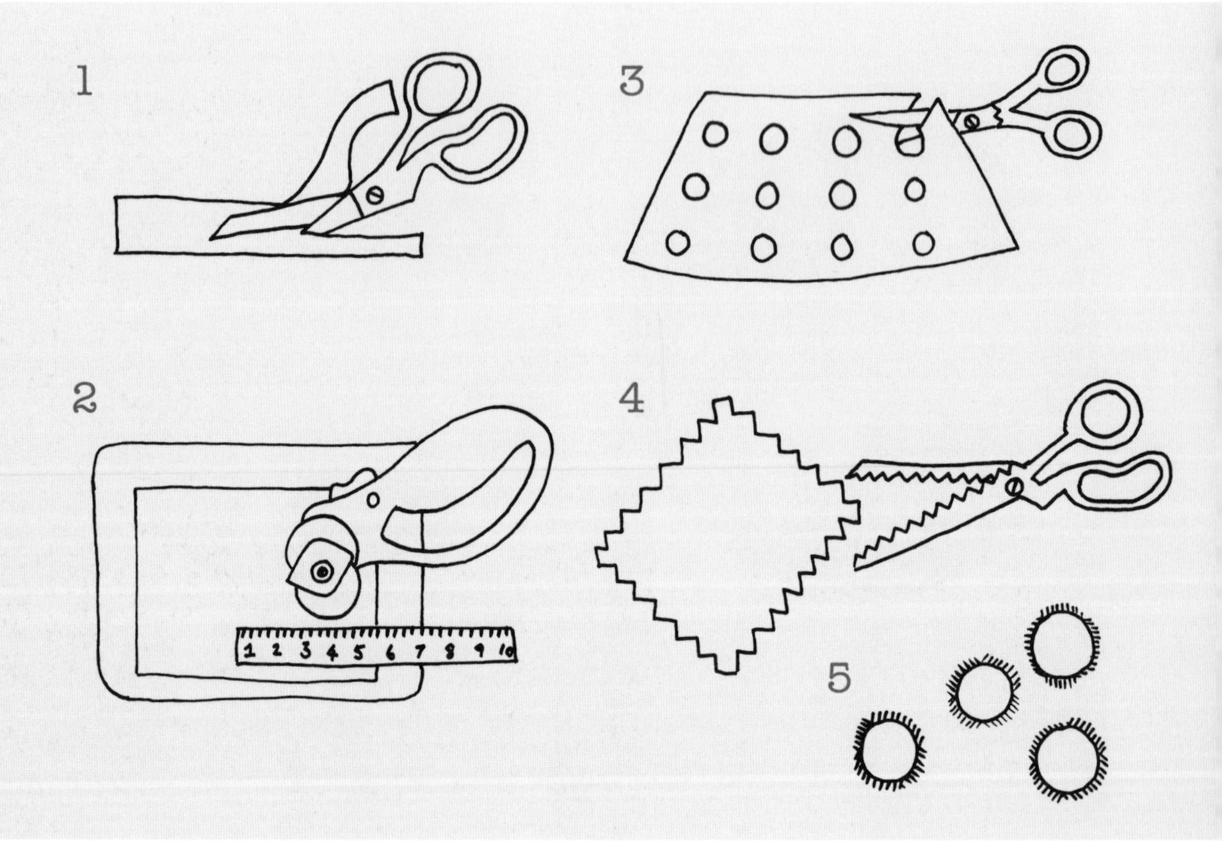

some contemporary designs incorporate frayed fabric edges; this works well with tough fabrics like denim that fray slightly (**5**).

### Stitching the shapes

The stitching technique you use to apply your cut shapes to the base fabric will depend on the nature of your design and its size. You can lay the shapes down in a variety of ways: very precisely, in neat geometric rows (**6a**); randomly scattered over the fabric (**6b**); or overlapped (**6c**). You can also layer one fabric on another, or cut away part of the top fabric to reveal the one beneath.

Once you have placed the shapes in their chosen positions, you can stitch them in place. Machine stitching is quickest and therefore best for larger pieces with multiple repeats. Fancy stitches are not needed; a simple straight stitch works well for most of the designs in this book. Hand stitching is more laborious but offers greater control with more fiddly designs or special fabrics. Make a decision based on whether you want an all-over repeating pattern for a larger piece of fabric or a special decoration for a smaller piece of fabric.

For an all-over repeating pattern it is quickest to use a straight stitch on the sewing machine and matching thread (**7**). You can make the stitching part of the surface decoration (**8**) or use a contrasting thread to vary the design.

For smaller projects or more fiddly designs, you may want to hand stitch the shapes using sewing or embroidery thread (**9**). Again, your choice of thread colour, matching or contrasting, depends on the effect you wish to achieve.

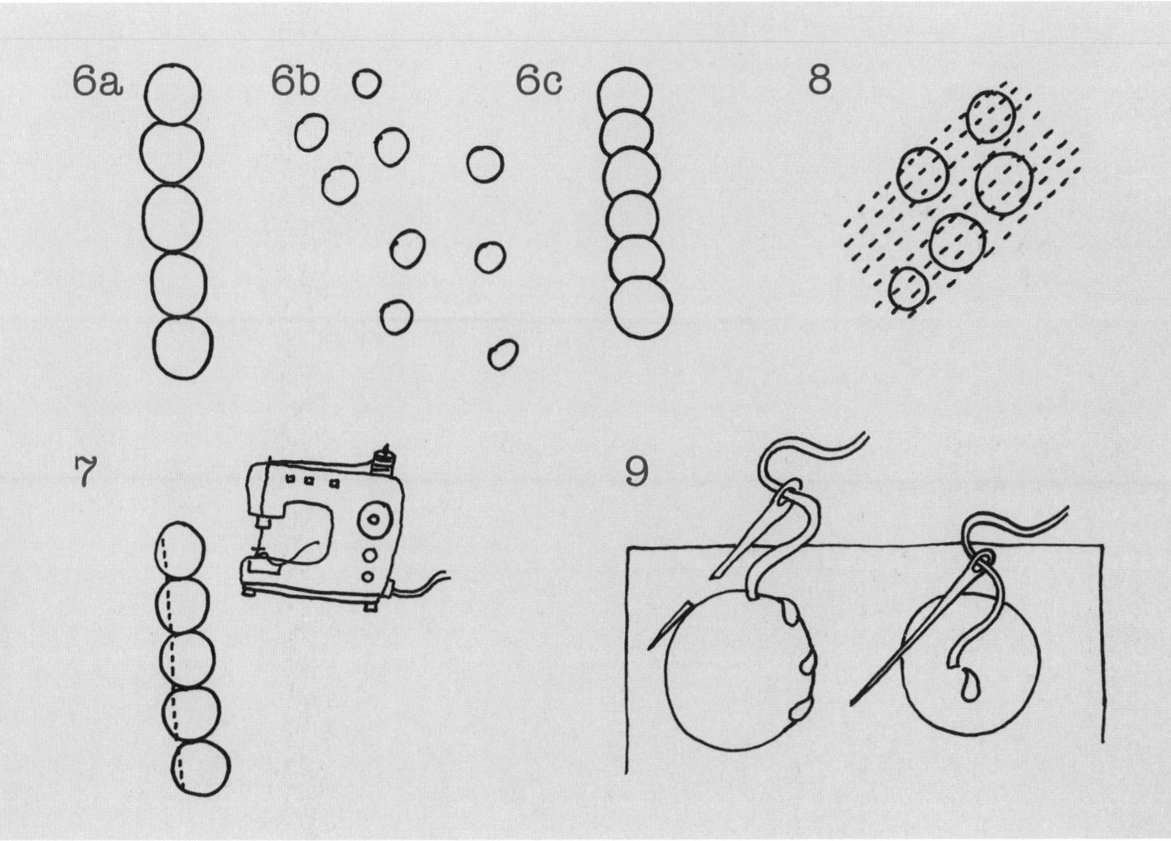

# tie belt

This belt is a simple rectangle that ties at the back (or front) with two cords. It is made by attaching flat circles of firm, non-fraying fabric to a strong non-fraying backing fabric. The belt shown here measures 56 x 8cm (22 x 3in).

**What you need**

Piece of thick, felted wool for the backing fabric to the depth and length required plus a slightly bigger piece of a firm non-fraying linen for the cut shapes; fabric-marking pencil; pre-formed circle template; ruler and set square; fabric glue; matching sewing thread; matching thick cord.

**1** Choose the size of your circle from the template (these measured 1.5cm/½in). Using a fabric-marking pencil, draw out a few rows of circles on the linen fabric.

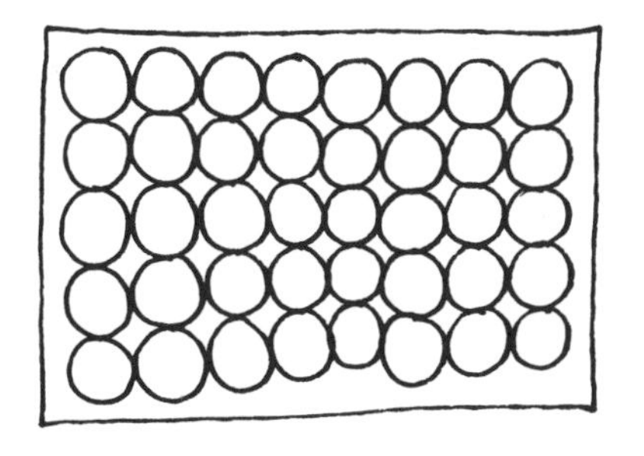

**2** Cut out a row of circles from the marked fabric.

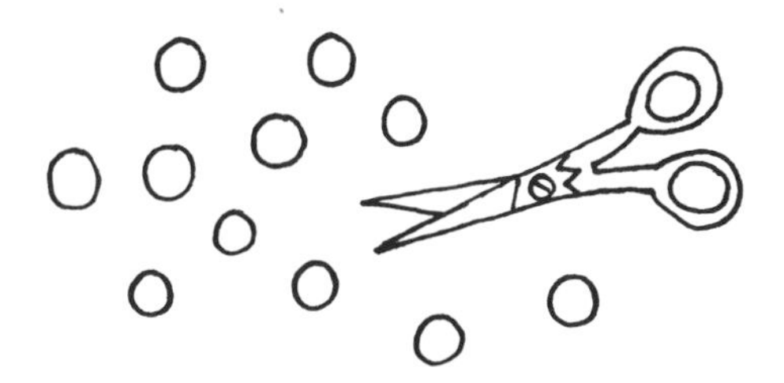

**3** Mark the shape of the belt base on the backing fabric with a fabric-marking pencil using a ruler and set square. Cut out the belt base. Start to lay the first column of circles down the right-hand side of the belt shape, so that one edge marries up with the edge of the fabric and the edges of the circles just touch each other. (Once you have laid down the first row, you can work out how many more circles you will need to cover the base; cut these out and keep them neat and flat, until ready to use.)

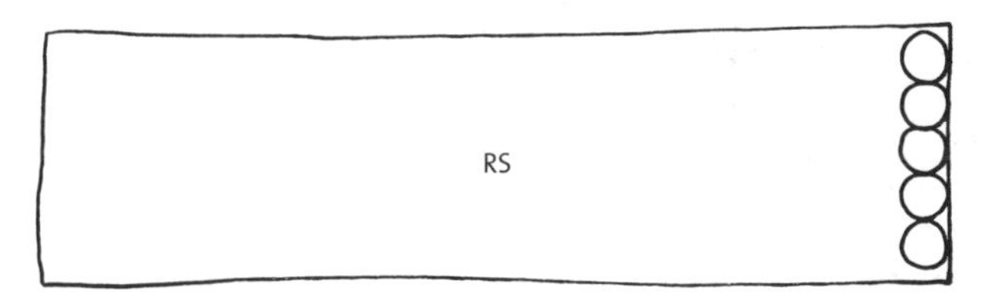


**4** Stick the circles down with a tiny dab of fabric glue. Machine stitch carefully down the first column of circles in a neat straight line on the left-hand side.

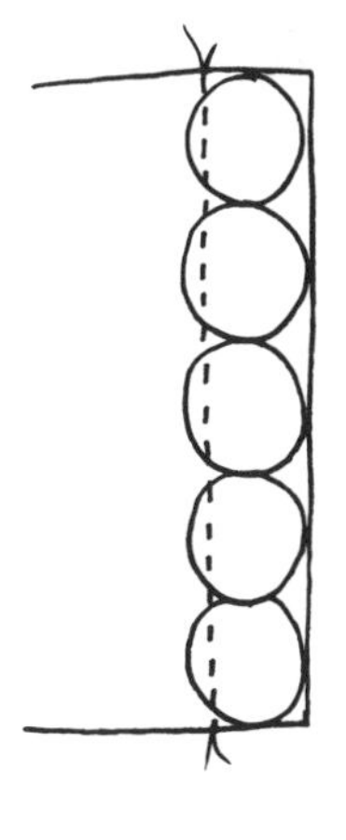

**5** When you have stitched the first column in place, position the next one so that each column of circles slightly overlaps the circles in the previous column, just enough to hide each line of previous stitching.

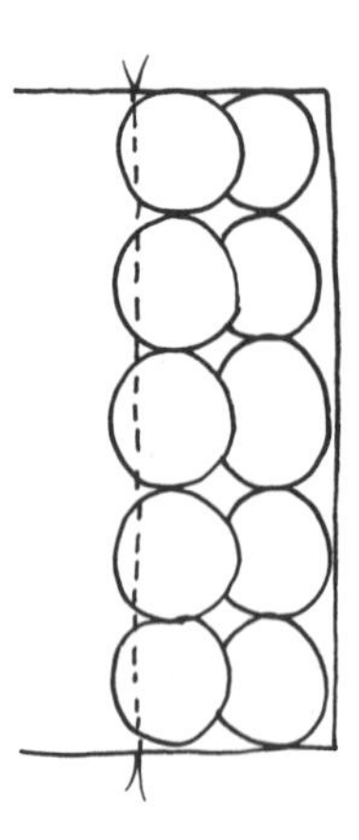

**6** Continue to create the overlapping columns of circles in this way, until you have covered the entire base of the belt. Trim each end of the base fabric of the belt to make a scallop shape, using the rows of circles as a guide.

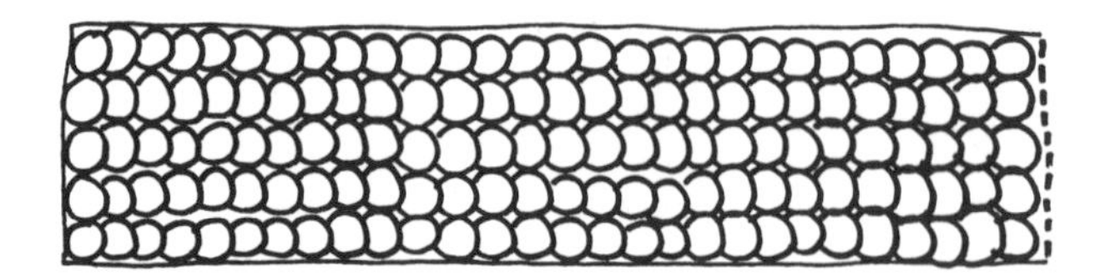

**7** To make the belt ties, one for each end of the belt, cut two matching lengths of cord (or fine strips from the surplus backing fabric) and stitch one end of each cord to the centre of each end of the belt. For a finishing detail, make a single knot in the other end of each cord.

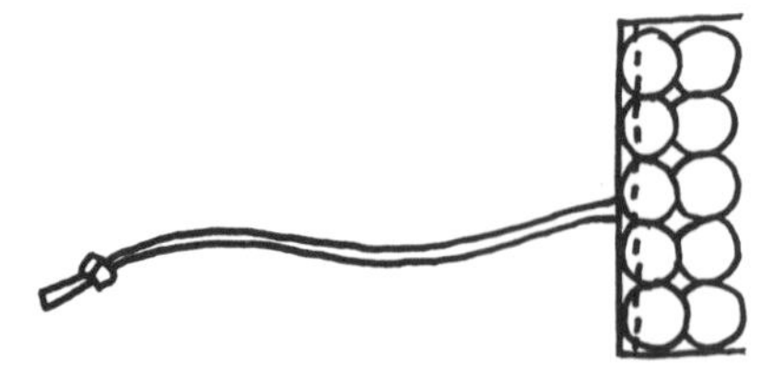

# place mats

This little mat employs a similar technique to the belt but here two sizes of circles are cut from printed and plain fabric and laid on top of each other in overlapping rows. Choose colours and patterns that complement each other. Fabrics with sheen or a finish that gives them a slightly polished, glossy appearance are ideal for the circles – I used a linen that had a special coating. The light catches the sheen on the circles, which gives a sense of movement to the mat with a three-dimensional effect. You can glue the circles to each other and to the base, but only use a tiny amount as you don't want the glue to appear on the right side of the fabric. This mat measures 36 x 32cm (14¼ x 12½in).

**What you need**

Piece of plain glazed linen fabric for the top (cut to the size required plus 1.5cm/½in seam allowance all around); contrasting wool felt for the base; plain and printed glazed linen for the circles (slightly more than the size of the mat); pre-formed circle template; fabric glue; contrasting and matching sewing thread.

**1** Decide on two sizes of circles (one in each fabric), the smaller ones to be positioned on top of the larger ones. Cut out enough circles in each size to cover the surface of the top fabric. Here, the larger circle measures 3cm (1¼in) in diameter and the smaller circle measures 2.5cm (1in) in diameter.

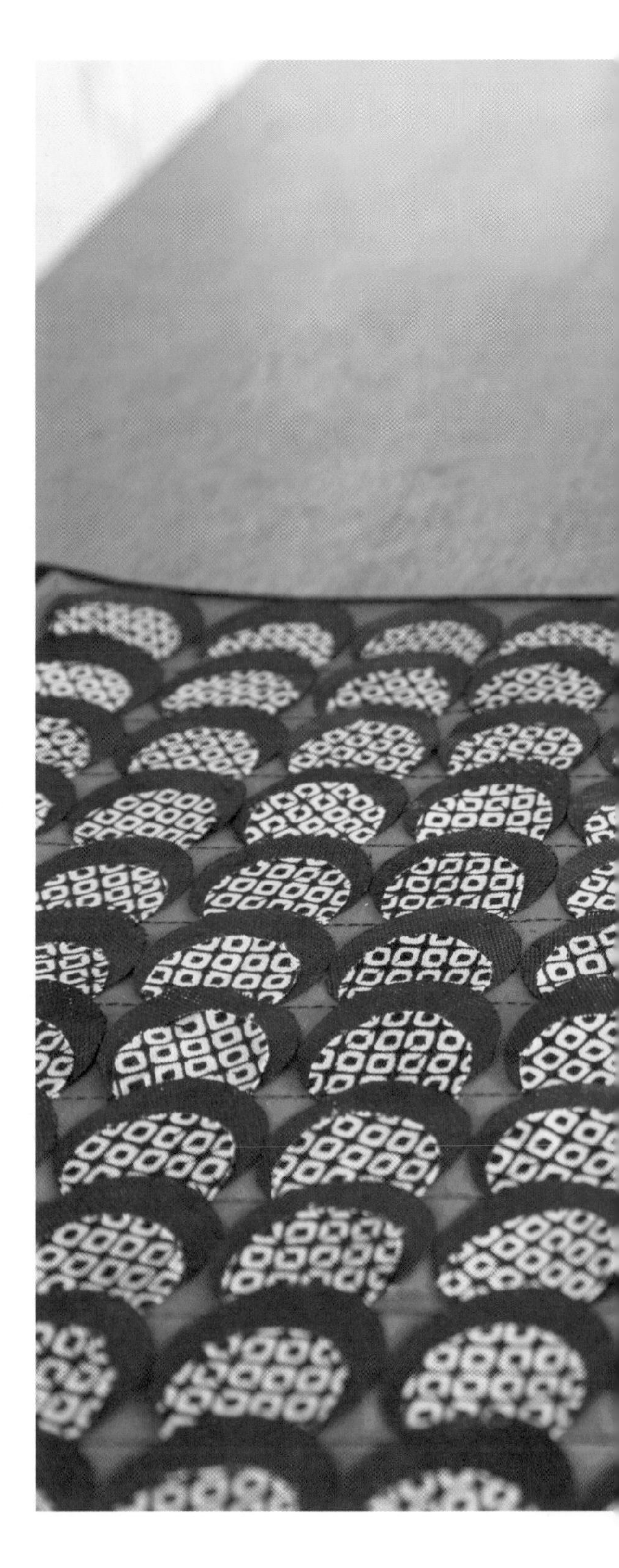

**2** Place each small circle on top of the larger one so that it touches the edge just on one side. Use a dab of fabric glue to keep the circles in place.

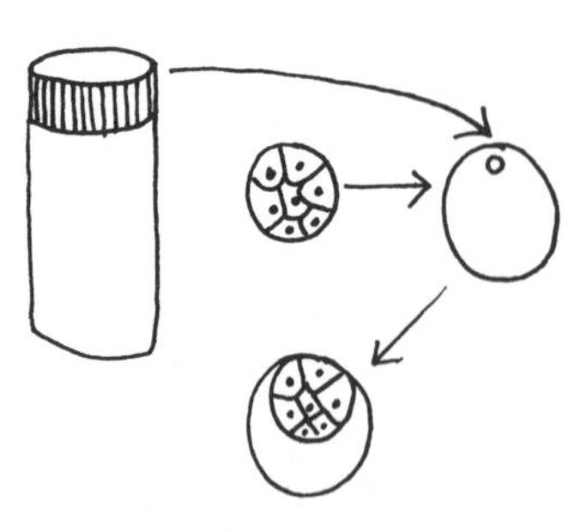

**3** Start to position the circles in a row along one long side of the top fabric, with the circles overlapping slightly. Leave the seam allowance at the edges. Use a dab of fabric glue to attach them. When you have positioned the first row, secure it with a line of machine stitching in contrasting thread, stitching over just the topmost edges of the circles.

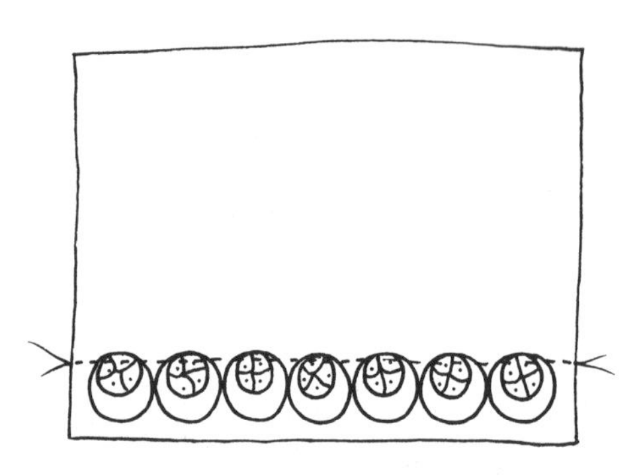

**4** Continue with the second row, positioning it so the edges slightly overlap the first row, to cover the previous line of stitching.

**5** Continue until all of the top fabric is covered in rows, apart from the seam allowance.

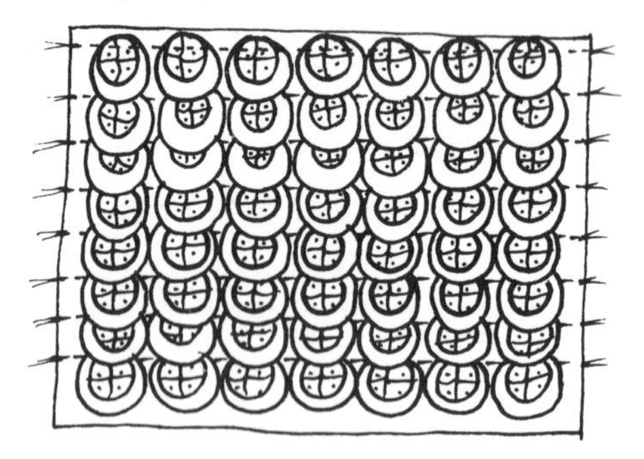

**6** Fold over the seam allowances along all four edges of the top fabric and press. Cut out a piece of contrasting wool felt slightly larger than the size of the mat. Pin the top to the base so a little of the wool border is revealed and topstitch together around all sides of the top in matching thread.

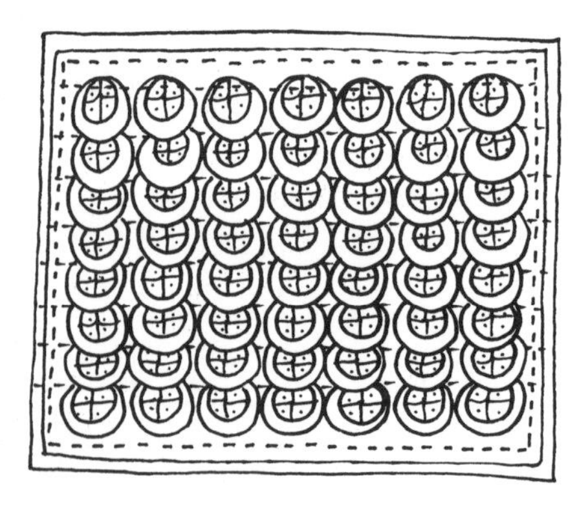

## ● black mat variation

I made this mat in the same way as the belt on page 18, but changed the dimensions and used a thick piece of wool felt for the base. The wool felt doesn't need to be hemmed because it doesn't fray; it also helps to make the mat heatproof. Glazed linen works well for the circles as you can wipe it clean.

If you have any printed cotton leftover from making circles for another project, use it to make some simple square napkins to complement the mats, like the one shown here.

Use a ruler and set square to mark out the chosen size of fabric square first and cut out. You can either overstitch the raw edges of the napkin with a zigzag stitch on the sewing machine or you can fold and press a hem, and topstitch it all around. For a fancier edging, pin the napkin fabric (wrong side down) to a piece of Stitch 'n' Tear fabric (see page 133) a little larger than the napkin (to act as a stabilizer for stitching). Close to the raw edge of the napkin, machine stitch a satin stitch border all around. Snip away the surplus napkin fabric outside the stitched border and remove the Stitch 'n' Tear fabric.

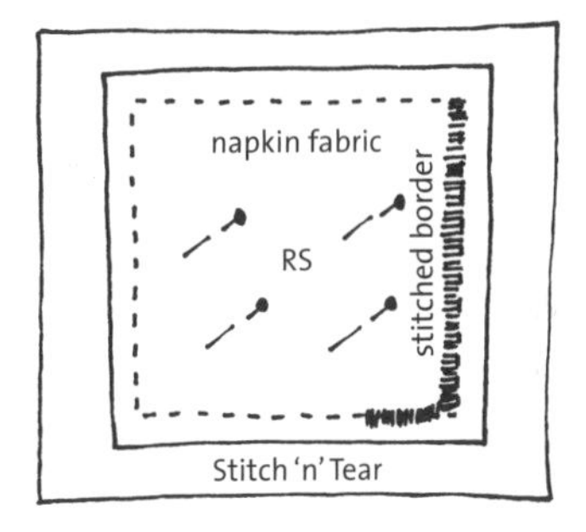

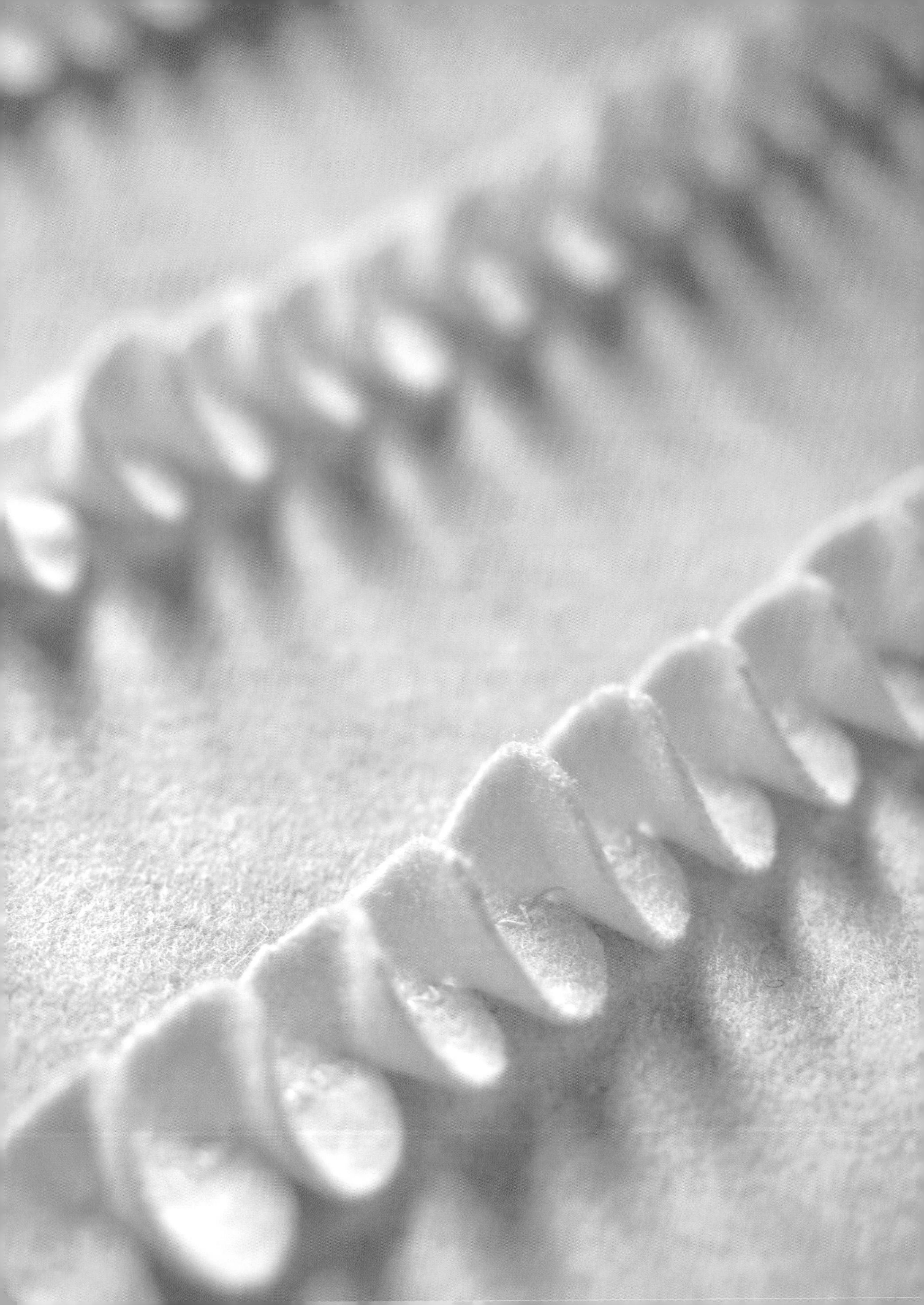

# folded shapes

This chapter shows you how to create interesting effects by cutting and folding small pieces of fabric to form three-dimensional shapes that can be applied to a base fabric or linked together in various ways. By treating fabric in much the same way as you would paper, you are following the basic principles of the Japanese paper-folding art of origami.

Whereas folds in paper are permanent once created, fabric requires more effort. To ensure that a fabric fold stays in place, you can use a pressing iron, which will create crisp folds on firmly woven cottons and linens, or, on softer fabrics, catch the folds with stitches.

Your choice of fabric will determine the style and form of the folds. You may prefer not to press the folds and, instead, allow them to curve naturally, which produces a much softer, more fluid effect. The most sculptural effects are created with thick, plain wools, but you can use printed cottons or linens to add spot decoration, stitching or bonding them to the thicker base fabric. (You can bond fabrics to each other with small dabs of fabric glue or by using bondaweb – a special glued fabric that is cut to the shape of the top fabric and ironed onto the back of it, enabling it to stick to the base fabric.) It is always a good idea to experiment, trying out different fabrics to see what happens. Don't be afraid of making mistakes as sometimes the best creative ideas come from errors – moments of serendipity that produce something special, allowing a new and innovative textile to come into being.

The samples I have included in this chapter are created by cutting out and folding varying fabric shapes and then either applying them to a base fabric with fabric adhesive or stitches, or connecting them to each other to create textile jewellery.

◀ Rows of cut and twisted circles in Melton wool are applied to the same base fabric, neatly stitched through the centres, creating softly sculptural rows of folds.

# design samples

This section covers a variety of simple designs, all of them easy to create. The cut and folded shapes can be repeated or just placed randomly on a base fabric. Once you start experimenting with different fabrics, shapes and arrangements, you will see that the possibilities are endless.

For example, you can use more than one piece of fabric at a time by cutting out a shape twice, in different fabrics. These fabrics can either be bonded together using fabric glue or bondaweb, or kept separately, giving you a wide range of choices. You could also think about mixing contrasting weights of fabric together: perhaps an open gauze with a densely woven fabric.

You can also have fun looking at different ways of working with the shapes. Try them on a foundation fabric or simply join the shapes together using a simple hand stitch to create a string of shapes. The results can make great textile jewellery pieces.

To create any fabric design that is professional-looking, it is important to draw out the shapes to a uniform size before cutting. Either create a stiff card or paper template or use one of the many pre-formed templates that are available, including squares, ovals and circles. These templates offer a quick and easy way to prepare multiple shapes.

If you are applying the shapes to a base fabric, you will need to mark out the positions for your folded shapes with a fabric-marking pencil. I like to create paper shapes first, so I can plan a design before deciding on their final size and position.

A

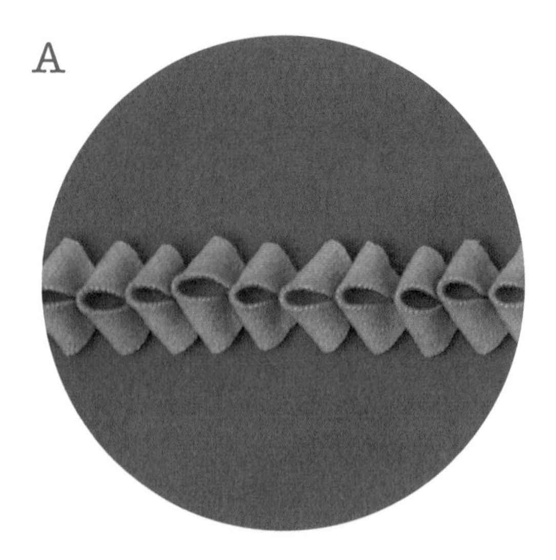

▲ **Sample A:** Small triangles have been cut out of a soft blue woollen fabric, then folded inwards and stitched to a similar red woollen base fabric. You can choose to use the same colours, or contrast them. This design works best in a fabric that folds gently without sharp creases.

B

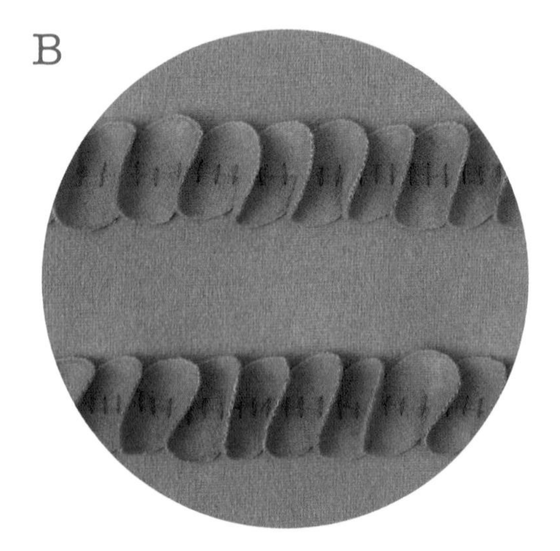

▲ **Sample B:** This sample uses the same fabric as Sample A but here the shapes have been changed to circles that are cut and twisted, and overlapped, to form a spiral pattern. The contrasting thread colour used to hold the shapes in place provides a neat accent.

C

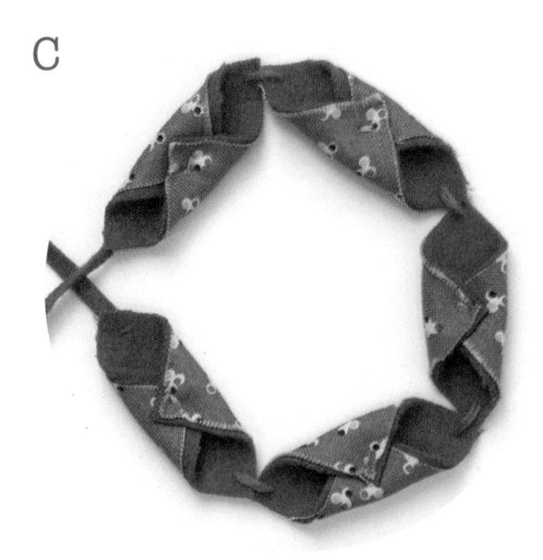

▲ **Sample C:** This sample uses a plain woollen fabric together with a patterned cotton (picking up the colour of the wool). Squares of the same size are cut from each fabric and bonded together before folding over opposite corners. The shapes are joined into a chain with a loose hand stitch.

E

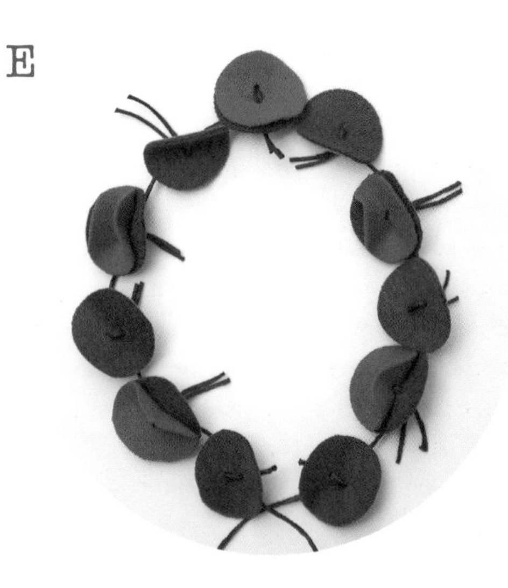

▲ **Sample E:** In this sample circles of smooth plain cotton are attached with paper thread to circles of felted woollen fabric. Some circles are folded in half so the chain becomes a mixture of circles and half circles.

D

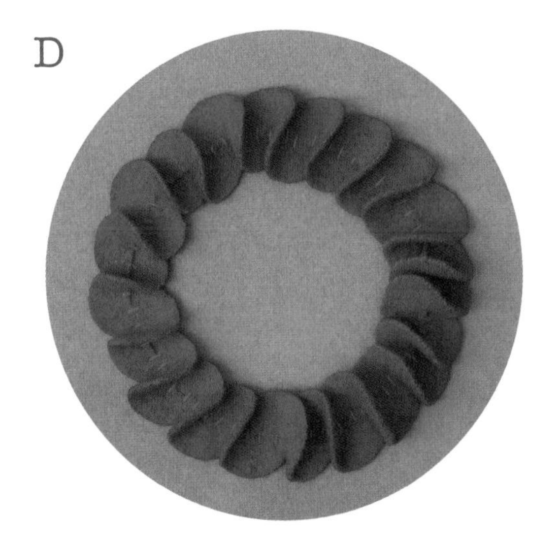

▲ **Sample D:** This variation on Sample B employs the same fabrics (soft Melton wools) and similar methods of construction, but in this case the circles are arranged in a ring rather than a row. To add a touch of pattern, you could bond a matching patterned fabric to the base fabric within the ring.

F

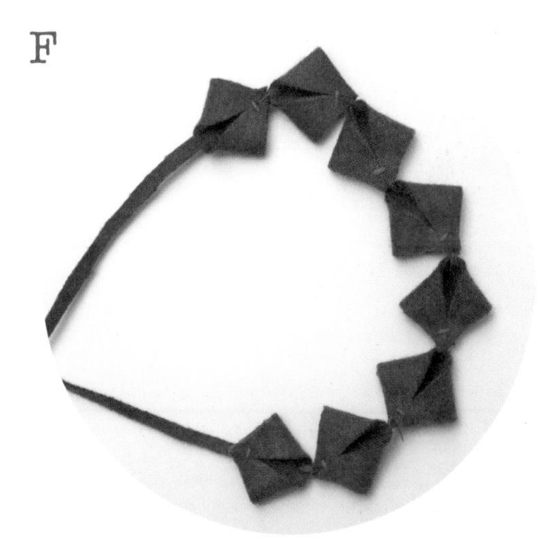

▲ **Sample F:** This is a variation on Sample A. It is created using the same fabric type and method. In this case, though, the folded triangles are held together with a contrasting coloured hand stitch, to form a chain as there is no backing fabric.

# how to fold shapes

First, make some simple design decisions. What colours are you going to use and what shape? Consider how you propose to use the shapes. Will they be attached to a base fabric for a bed throw or cushion, or used on their own as an item of jewellery? Your fabrics and colours will be determined by these choices.

**Cutting and folding the shapes**

Mark out your shapes on the straight grain of the fabric using a template, such as a pre-formed circle template, and a fabric-marking pencil (**1**). If you are not using a template, you will need to measure the shapes carefully using tools such as a compass or set square, so your shapes are identical and symmetrical. Then cut these out carefully using the appropriate cutting tool (**2**).

Small circles can be cut with a revolving hole punch. Larger circles are best cut out using small embroidery scissors, which give you more control than dressmaking shears. Rectangles are best cut out using the latter, as this enables smooth straight

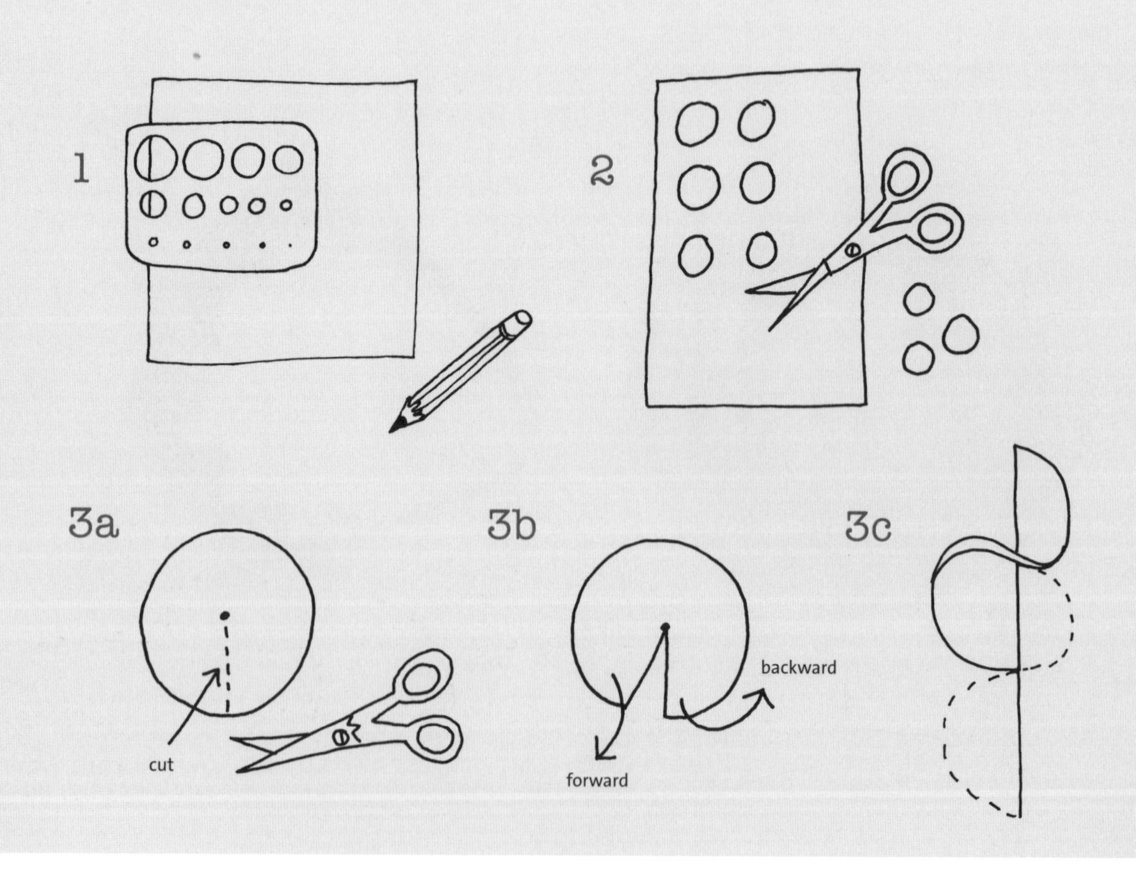

lines to be cut out easily, although you may find it easier to cut strips with dressmaking shears and then use a small pair of embroidery scissors to cut the strips into squares or rectangles.

To make the folded circles for the projects in this chapter, using small embroidery scissors, cut from the edge to the centre of each circle (**3a**). Pull one side of the circle towards you and the other to the back (**3b**) and then place the straight edge onto the marked line of the base fabric (**3c**).

To cut triangles, fold a square in half diagonally, press and cut along the diagonal fold (**4a**). To make folded triangles, fold the two opposite points of each triangle inwards to meet the top point (**4b**). Use a tiny amount of fabric glue to hold the folded shape in place before it is stitched (**4c**).

**Attaching the shapes to the base fabric**

You can use a small amount of fabric glue to hold the prepared shapes in place on your base fabric before you stitch them to it, using hand or machine stitching. When attaching a row of circles to the base fabric, place the next twisted circle adjacent to the first, continuing along the marked line until complete, holding each in place with a little fabric glue.

On a sewing machine, use either straight or zigzag stitch (**5a**), and stop and start the machine to stitch only through the centres of the circles. If you prefer to use hand stitches, just make two or three stab stitches (**5b**) to attach the circles. When worked in a contrasting thread, the hand stitches have a lovely hand-rendered quality.

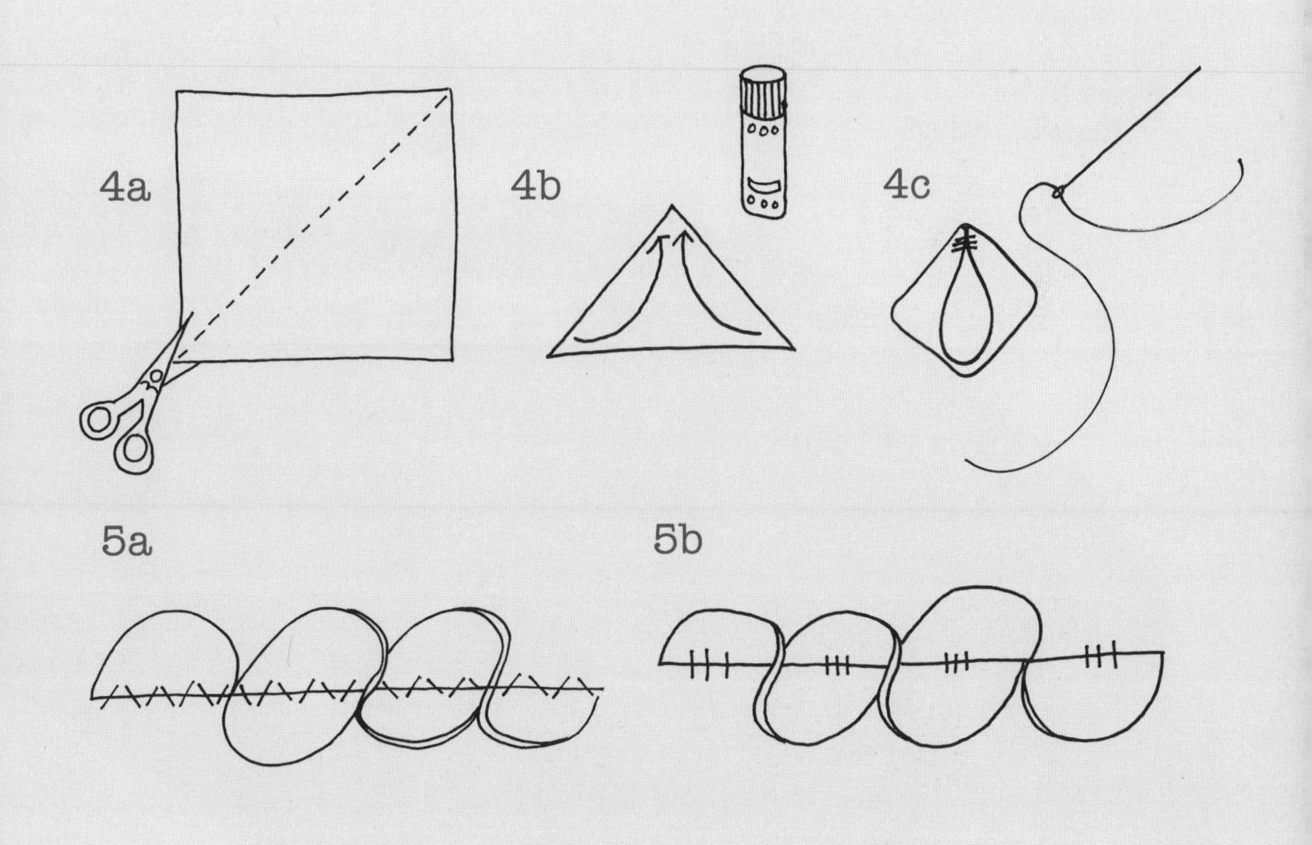

# ● bed throw

The narrow throw shown here is meant for the end of the bed, but you can adapt the design to any size. You can also position the fabric circles as you wish, making them either all the same size or varying sizes. The fabric for this throw is a felted woollen cloth. It does not need to be lined because it does not fray when cut. To determine the ideal size and placement of your circles, make some out of paper and experiment first. Here, the little circles for the rings measure 2.5cm (1in) in diameter; the big circles for the rows are 3.5cm (1½in) in diameter. The throw measures 60 x 180cm (24 x 72in).

**What you need**

Felted woollen fabric for the base to the size required; a third of that amount of similar fabric in a contrasting colour for the circles; set square and ruler; fabric-marking pencil; compass or pre-formed circle template; sewing thread; fabric glue; hand-sewing needle.

**Making the throw**

**1** Cut the base fabric to the required size, taking great care to cut it straight using a ruler and set square and dressmaking shears (see page 10). Using a fabric-marking pencil, draw lines to mark the position for the two long rows of circles on each side of the throw, approximately 15cm (6in) from the edge.

**2** Using a compass, prepare paper templates for the large ring shapes.

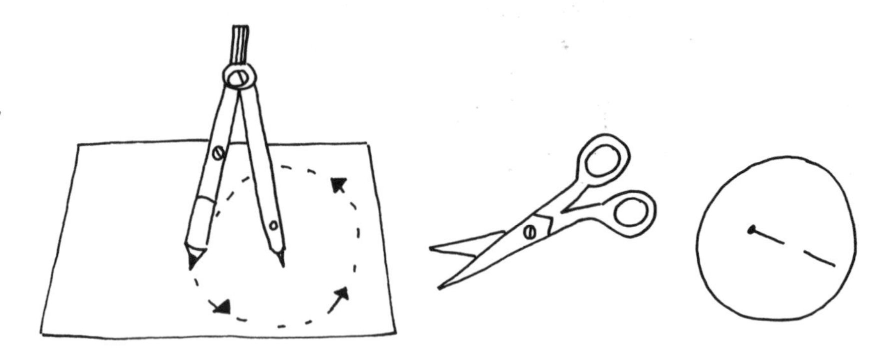

**3** Lay the base fabric out flat and position the paper templates for the rings along the centre, between the lines marked in Step 1. When happy with the position, draw round the templates to mark the fabric with a fabric-marking pencil.

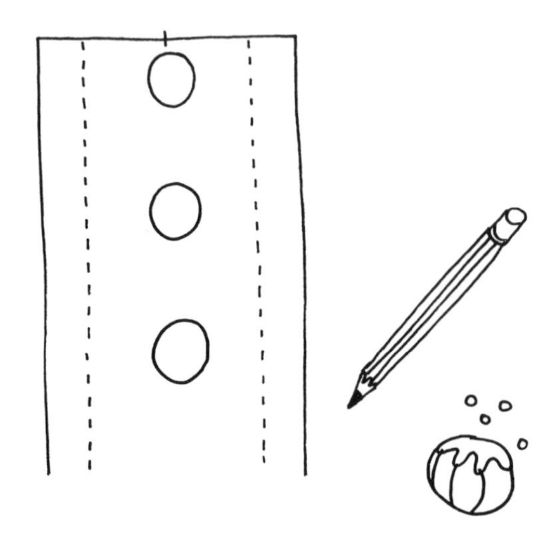

**4** Prepare your cut circle shapes (see page 30) for the long rows and for the circles, either using a compass or pre-formed circle template for the two sizes. Twist the circles (see page 31) and place them in the chosen positions, using a small dab of glue.

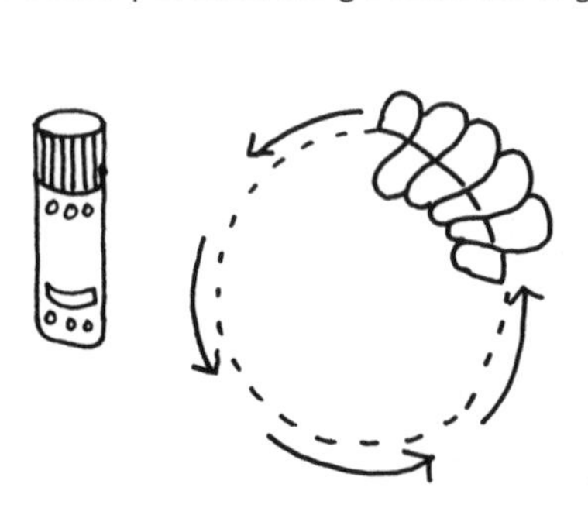

**5** Stitch the long rows in position using either machine zigzag stitch (see page 31) or a few stab stitches in the centre of each small circle.

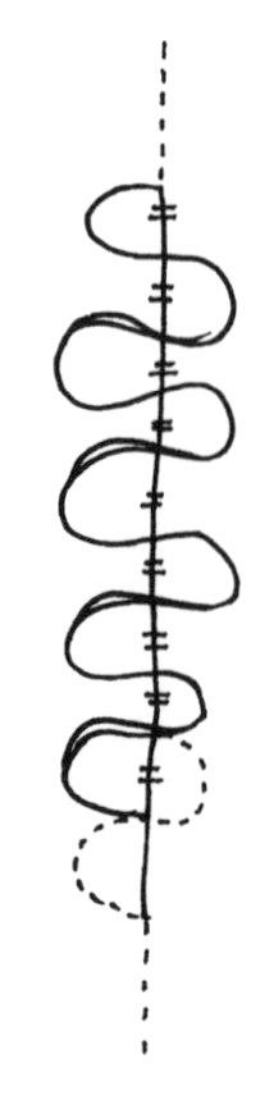

**6** Stitch the smaller twisted circles in position on the large ring shapes, using the same stitching method that you used for the long rows in Step 5.

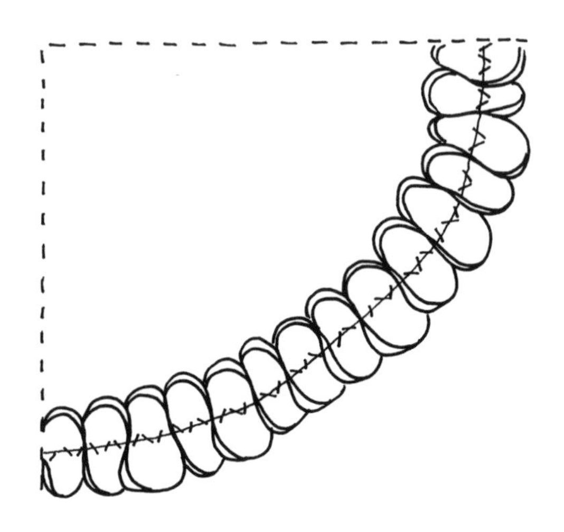

# circle necklace

This necklace is based on design Sample E on page 29. Each circle shown measures 3cm (1¼in) in diameter. Here 11 pairs of circles have been created from two plain felts and one patterned fabric. Where two felt circles are paired together, they have been left unbonded to add an extra dimension to the design. A length of paper thread serves as the base for the necklace and the tie. Some of the pairs of circles have been folded in half. Experiment and create your own necklace as desired.

**What you need**

Length of paper thread sufficient for the length of necklace required, plus 10cm (4in) for trimming and tying; very small amount of two colours of plain felt and one patterned fabric; fabric glue; revolving hole punch.

**Making the necklace**

**1** Cut out the number of circles required for the design in the chosen fabrics and bond each pair of patterned and felt fabric circles using a small amount of fabric glue.

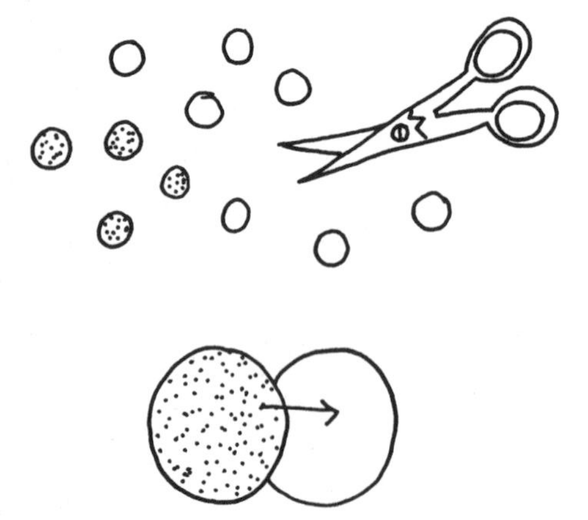

**2** Fold each bonded circle or pair of felt circles in half and cut out a small hole in the centre using a revolving hole punch, so that you have two holes when the circle is opened out.

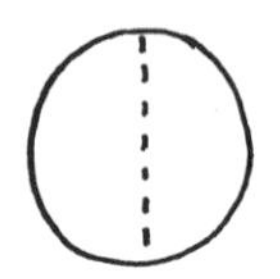

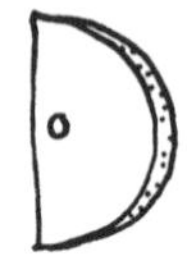

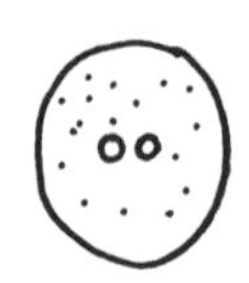

**3** Double over a short length of paper thread and push the folded end through the lined-up holes in the folded circle.

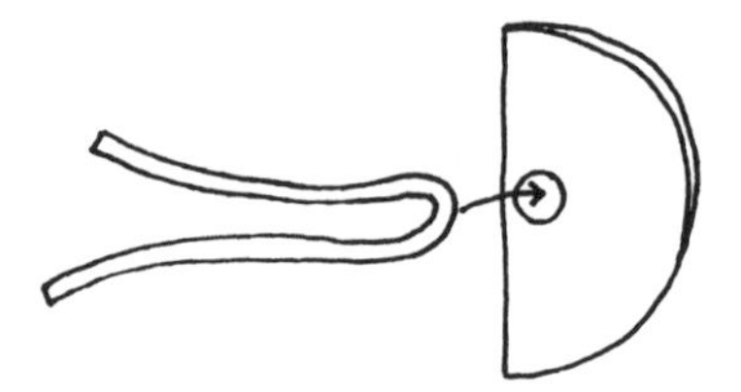

**4** Wrap the loop around the necklace thread, and thread the ends back through the loop and pull tight. Fold some pairs of circles in half before threading through.

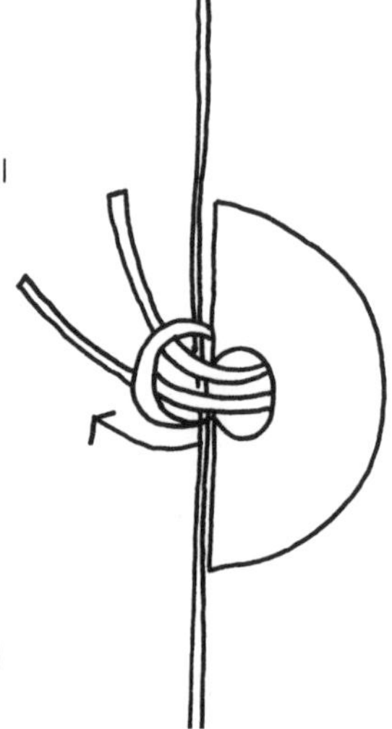

**5** Trim the necklace thread length to suit and knot the ends to tie.

# triangles necklace variation

This simple variation is based on the triangle design Sample F on page 29, but using felted fabric to create the cord and tie fastening. To make it, cut out triangles and create the 3-D shapes (see page 31). Glue and then stitch each shape to secure. Lay the triangles down on a flat surface facing in the same direction (so that you can see the length they make). Carefully hand stitch each 3-D shape to the next one, stitching the top of one shape to the base of the next. Cut two narrow strips of felted fabric to use as a cord and fastening. Attach one end of each cord to one end of the strip of triangles.

Here the triangles are linked with a contrasting coloured stitch or you could use a metal circle. Tie the ends to close or make a button fastener.

### TIP

To make a decorative button fastener for your necklace, fold over one end of one strip of cord fabric to form a loop to match the size of your chosen button. Stitch the loop in place. Sew the button on the other end of the strip.

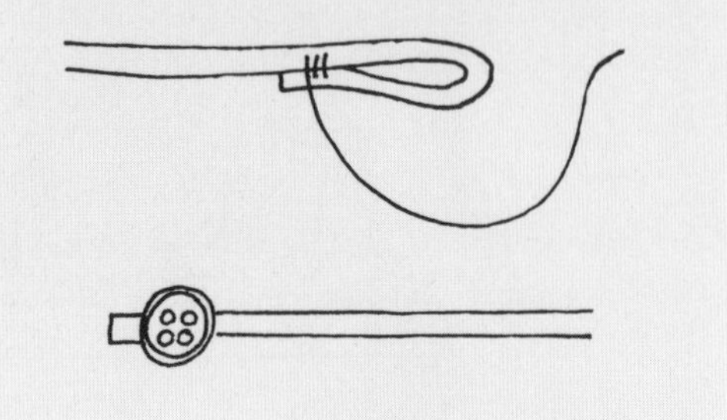

# pleating

Pleating is a decorative way to manipulate fullness in fabric. Pleats can be made from a wide variety of fabrics and each fabric will have its own distinctive characteristics when handled – fluid and soft in wools and silks and crisp and neat in linens and cottons, for example. Your choices will depend on the project you have in mind. Pleats make a neat edging on fabric pieces, such as throws and cushions, but they can also be used to create exciting textural qualities in the fabric itself.

There are two basic kinds of pleats: flat pleats and projecting pleats. Flat pleats are parallel folds of fabric laid down side by side. This type of pleat includes knife pleats, box pleats and inverted pleats. Projecting pleats are folds lifted from the surface of the fabric and arranged so they stand out from the fabric itself. This type of pleat includes pinch pleats, organ pleats and cartridge pleats.

Pleats can be produced in two ways, either by hand or industrially by machine. The amount of fabric required for pleating is generally three times the finished length. Therefore a pleated section that needs to be 10cm (4in) long will initially require 30cm (12in) of fabric (plus seam allowance).

Pleats are generally held in place with some form of stitching; you can also stitch decoratively on the pleats themselves. Fabric can be pleated both vertically and horizontally to create an interesting sculptural effect with raised patterns.

◀ Narrow pleats have been stitched vertically on fine wool fabric and then groups of similar fine pleats have been stitched horizontally across them, creating an attractive double fold where they meet.

# ● design samples

The design samples shown here include pleats in a range of different fabrics, plain and patterned, held in place using both machine and hand stitching. The way you stitch will, in part, depend on practicality. A larger project may demand machine stitching, whereas a smaller one can be worked by hand; hand stitching can give the finished piece a more luxurious, delicate feel than stitching by machine. You can also bring variety into your designs by mixing fabric types, for example a gauzy, finely pleated fabric applied to a woollen base, as well as colours and patterns.

I have created two all-over pleated projects from the design samples – a cushion from a shot silk using Sample F and a belt from printed and plain cottons using Sample C. Both are machine stitched. Pleated fabrics also lend themselves well to decorative trims, such as pleated borders on cushions or throws.

When choosing fabrics for your designs, think carefully about the way they will be used and the style of the pleated folds, so that you can get the best sculptural or textural effects. For example, the play of light created by the folds in the silk fabrics of Samples E and F is part of the effect.

The precise nature of pleating requires a certain amount of calculation, firstly to get the pleats to fall as you wish and secondly to estimate the amount of fabric required. Remember, too, that pleats create a triple layer of fabric, which can be quite bulky when stitching, so you may need to choose finer fabrics than you would normally.

A

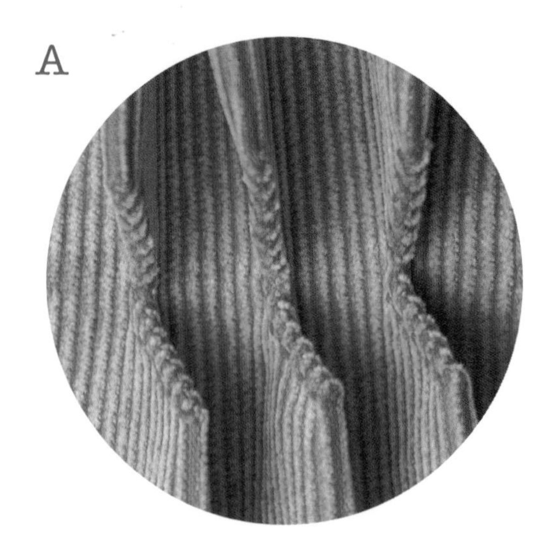

▲ **Sample A:** Here a series of projecting pleats has been created on a fine cotton corduroy fabric. To create the cut-away effect, a triangular section of the pleat is marked out, machine stitched and then cut away. This kind of effect works best with a fabric that can hold its shape well.

B

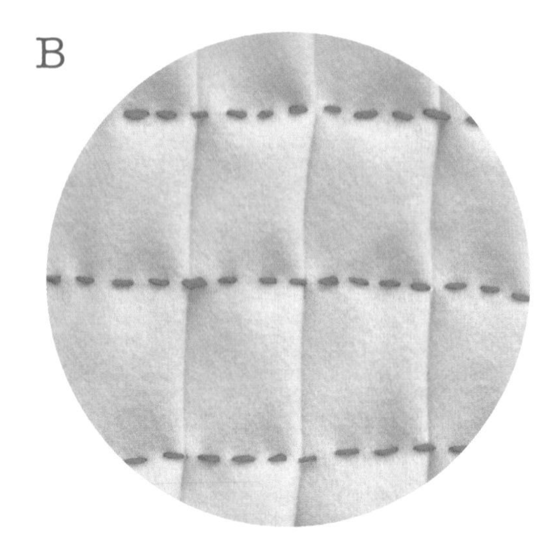

▲ **Sample B:** A cream Melton wool has been folded into a series of same-sized knife pleats. The fabric has not been pressed so the pleats form gentle soft folds. Hand stitching in contrasting thread across the fabric at regular intervals creates a design feature and holds the pleats in place.

C

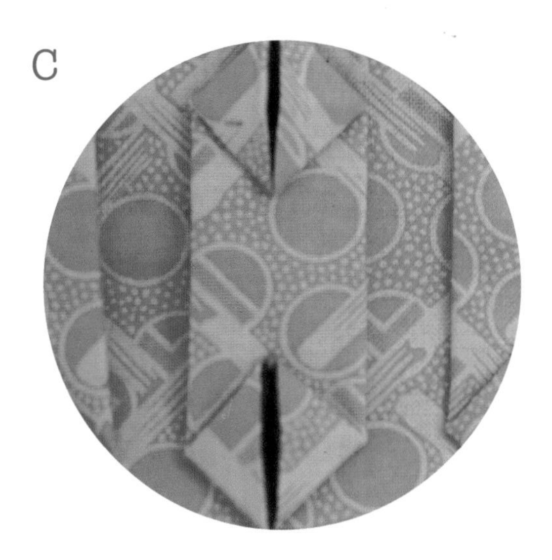

▲ **Sample C:** A vintage cotton print has been lined with a fine black cotton and treated as one fabric. The fabric is then box pleated; the ends of the pleats form origami-type folds that reveal the black cotton lining.

E

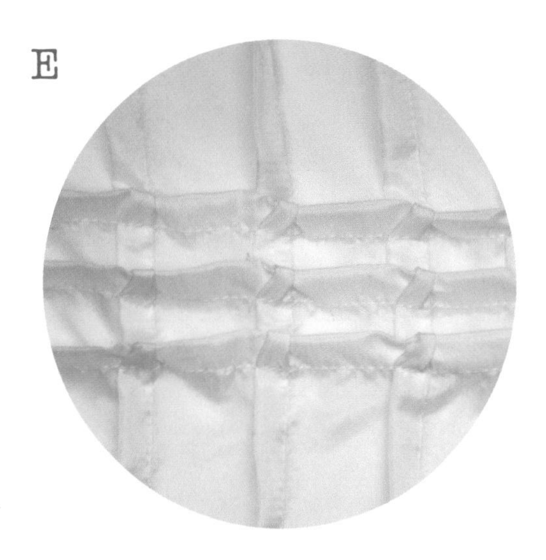

▲ **Sample E:** In this sample a fine silk is first pleated vertically and then horizontally, in groups of three, creating a knotted effect where the pleats cross. You can vary the number of pleats and their spacing to produce different effects.

D

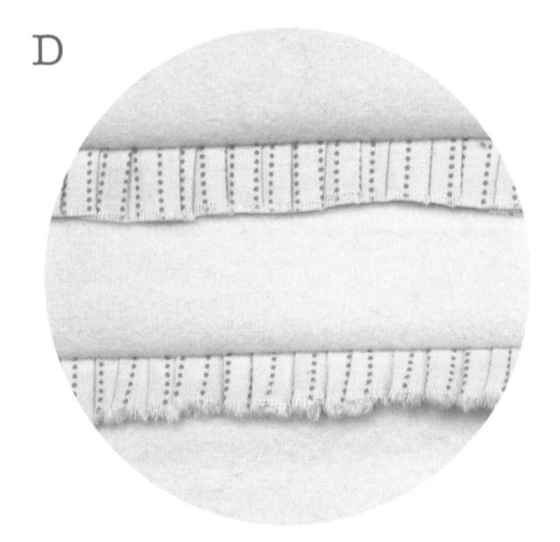

▲ **Sample D:** Here an orange print fabric has been folded into randomly sized pleats and stitched at the top to a cream wool fabric. The pleats have been applied in rows and steam pressed to retain their folds. This technique works well if using contrasting fabric and colours.

F

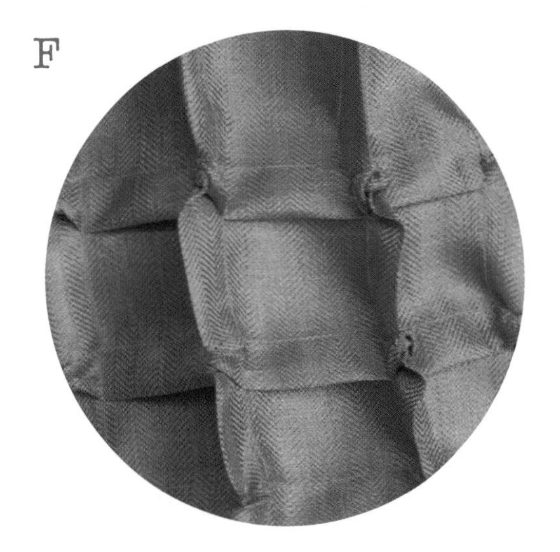

▲ **Sample F:** Similar to Sample E, but here the pleats are stitched at regular intervals to create a criss-cross pattern that knots where the pleats cross. It works well on both crisp and soft fabrics, but particularly on silks that catch the light.

# how to pleat

Before you begin, remember that you will usually need about three times as much fabric as the size of your finished piece when incorporating pleats. Always iron out creases from your fabric before you start and if you are making precise measured pleats, then use the appropriate measuring tools to ensure that your pleats are a consistent size.

First decide on the form and size of your pleats. A good way to work this out is to prepare your pleats in paper first. You can then unfold the paper and put pencil marks on each of the fold lines. When working the pleats in fabric, hold them in place with pins or tacking stitches before stitching into place.

**Making the pleated design samples**

For Sample A, a series of projecting pleats are pinned and stitched in place and a triangular shape (**1a**) marked on each fold of the fabric (you can use a triangular template) and the edges of the shape stitched first using a straight machine stitch or

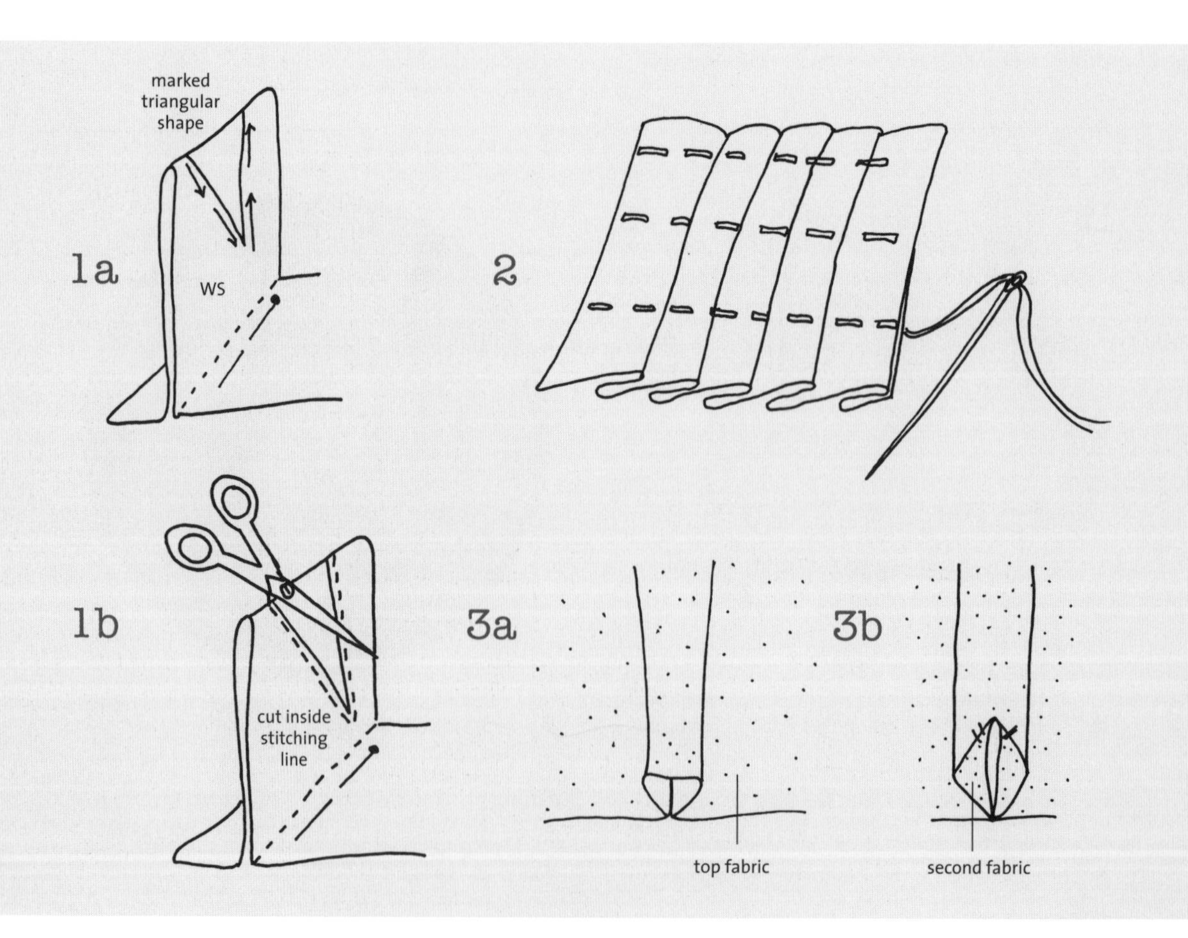

small hand running stitch. All the triangular shapes are cut out inside the stitching line (**1b**).

Sample B is made from knife pleats on the right side of the fabric. These pleats are folded and pinned in place while a hand-sewn straight stitch is worked across the pleats, repeated in regular rows across the fabric (**2**).

Sample C is made using box pleats (see page 53). In this sample, two different fabrics are used as one, stitched right sides together into a large rectangle, then turned right sides out. A series of small, neat box pleats are folded along the entire length, pressed and stitched in place (**3a**). To create further interest, you can reveal the second fabric by folding the tops of the pleats inwards towards the centre, held in place with a small hand stitch (**3b**).

Sample D incorporates loosely-pleated fabric strips (**4a**) in between strips of base fabric. The pleated strip is held in place using a straight stitch on the machine. Carefully insert your pleated fabric in between two pieces of base fabric (**4b**). With right sides together and with raw edges aligned, sew a straight stitch across the bottom. Open out and press, pressing the pleats flat.

For the criss-cross pleats in Samples E and F, a series of fine projecting pleats are stitched first vertically (**5a**) and then horizontally across the fabric (**5b**). The spacing of the horizontal pleats creates the different patterns. At each point where the pleats cross, pull the overlapping fabric so that it folds back on itself to create distinctive little knots of fabric.

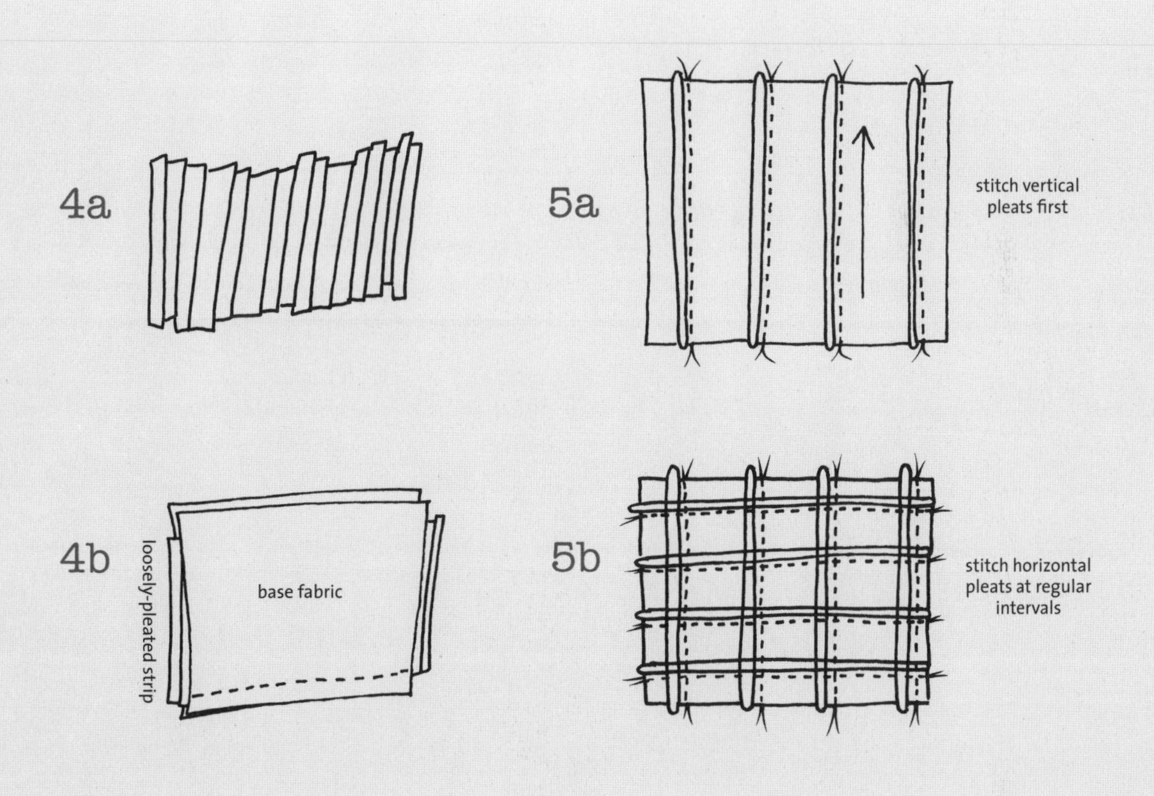

# cushion cover

This criss-cross pleat formation looks complex but is surprisingly easy to execute. The cushion here, made out of Habutai silk that catches the light beautifully, measures 30cm (12in) square and has 11 rows of pleats in each direction.

**What you need**

Piece of fabric 99cm (39in) square for the front, plus two pieces each 33 x 23cm (13 x 9in) for the back flaps; matching sewing thread; fabric-marking pencil; ruler; 30cm (12in) square cushion pad.

**Making the front**

**1** Press your fabric and carefully mark the pleat positions on opposite sides with a fabric-marking pencil, starting 1.5cm (½in) in on all sides to allow for seam allowance. Mark pleats at repeating intervals of 3cm (1¼in) followed by 2cm (¾in).

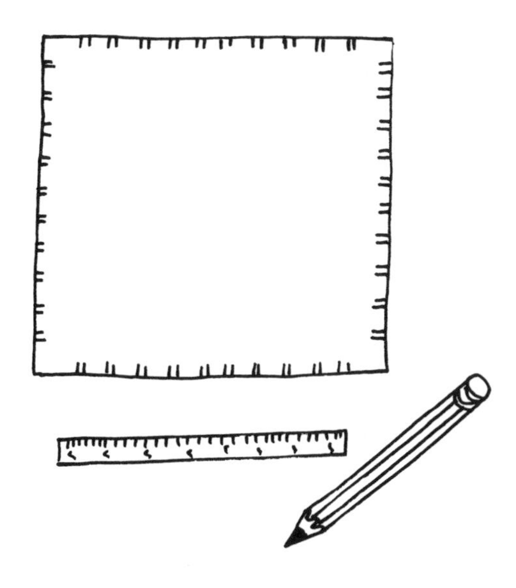

**2** Working across the top of the fabric, fold and pin the 2cm (¾in) pleats in place.

**3** Stitch down each vertical pleat.

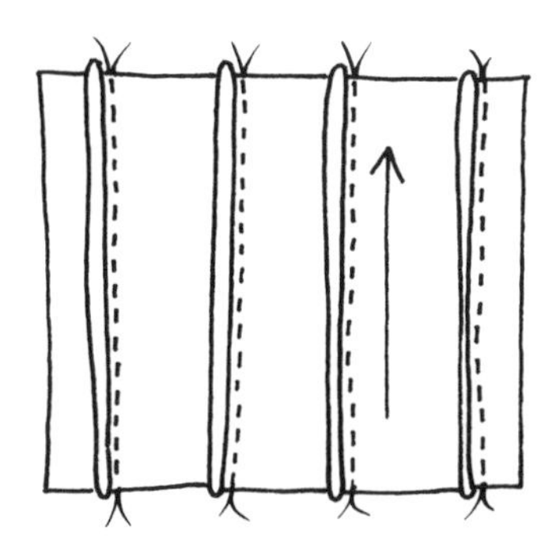

**4** Working down the side of the fabric, fold and pin the horizontal pleats to complete a grid-like formation of pleats across the cushion.

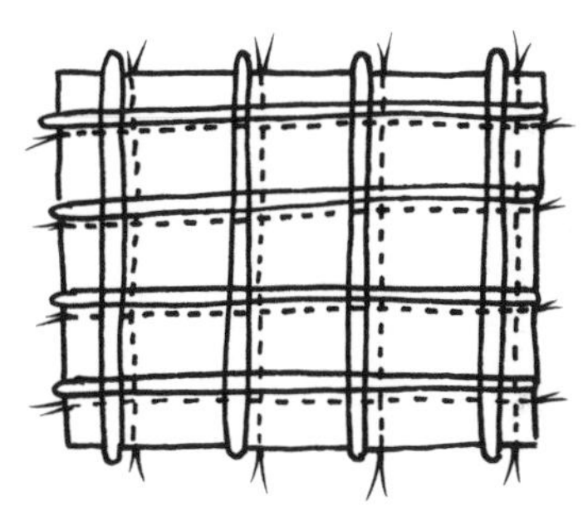

**5** Where the pleats cross each other, pull back the little flap of fabric to make the knotted effect.

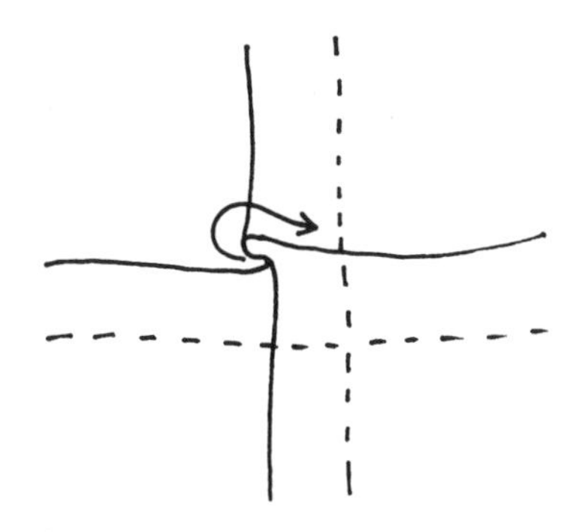

**Making the back**

**6** Press both back pieces of fabric. Fold over the raw edges on the long sides of each of the pieces twice to produce a neat edge. Top stitch in place and press.

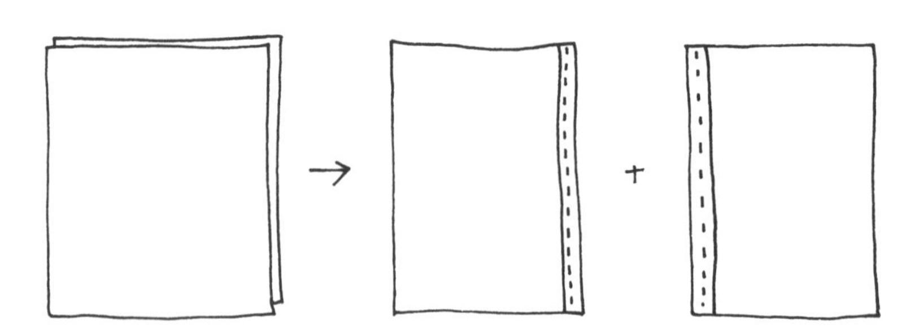

**7** With the pleated fabric right side up, place the two shorter edges of the fabric to opposite sides of the cushion font. These two pieces will overlap a little.

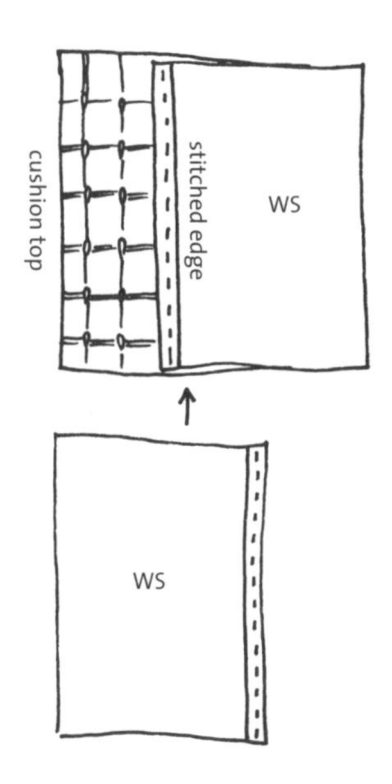


**8** Pin the edges. Machine a straight stitch around the edges, leaving 1.5cm (½in) seam allowance. Press the seams open and turn the cushion cover right sides out. You can now insert the cushion pad through the open flaps on the back.

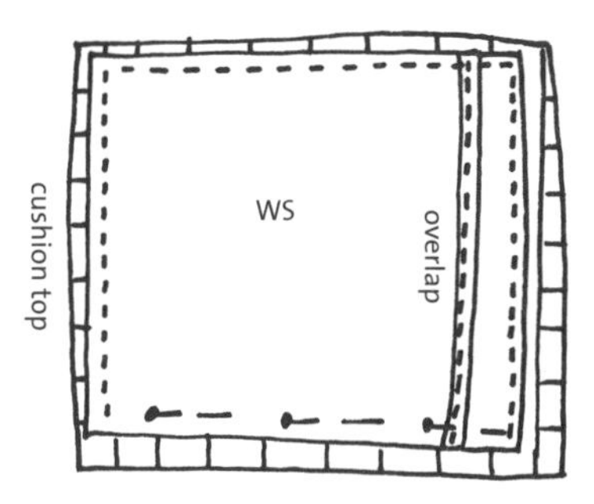


## cream cushion variation

This cushion was created from Sample F on page 43. I used a very fine cream woollen fabric, but if you want to make a matching pair with the orange cushion, use the same Habutai silk. You will need to plan your pleat positions carefully, with evenly spaced pleats for the vertical pleats, and two groups of three pleats for the horizontal ones, taking care to place the horizontal ones equidistant from the cushion sides.

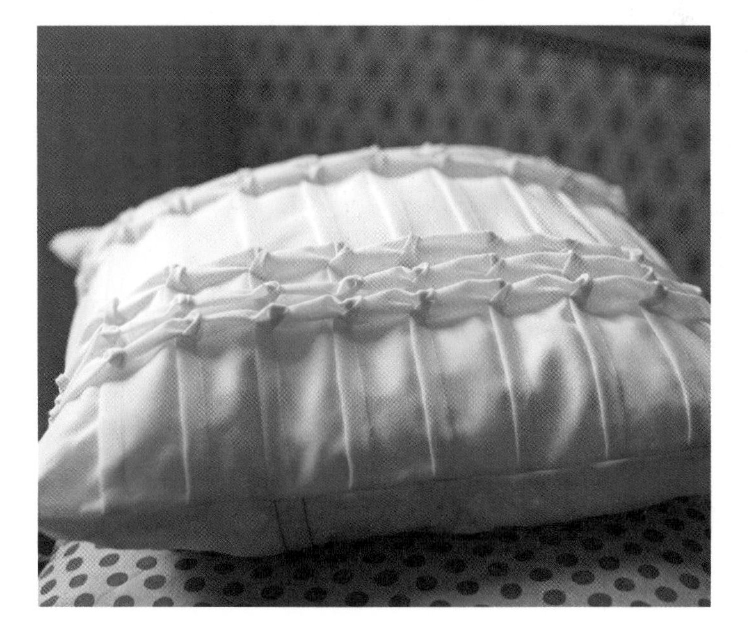

# pleated origami belt

This belt has a strong Oriental feel. The contrast of a vintage print on the front and a plain fabric on the back in conjunction with the folding techniques, creates a bold geometric design. When you make the box pleats and fold the tops down into a triangular shape, the contrasting plain fabric is revealed at the top and bottom of each pleat. To finish the belt, look for an appropriate vintage buckle. You will need to work out how long you want the belt to be. The one here measures 86 x 7cm (34 x 2½in) and the buckle measures 7 x 4cm (2¾ x 1½in). You can create slightly smaller or larger pleats to adjust them to the length required. These measure 2.5cm (1in) wide.

### ● ● ● TIP

To avoid having to work out the maths to get the belt to fit, simply make it longer than you need, trim off the surplus, fold the ends into a triangle and turn under the belt buckle. Fold in the raw ends and stitch in place on the back.

**What you need**

Two lengths of fabric, one printed and one plain, three times the length of your proposed belt, plus 1.5cm (½in) seam allowance, by the width of the belt, plus 1.5cm (½in) seam allowance; matching sewing thread; ruler and set square; belt buckle.

**Making the belt**

**1** Mark out and carefully cut the two fabrics to the required size. Pin right sides together along the two long sides and sew a straight stitch seam, taking a 1.5cm (½in) seam allowance.

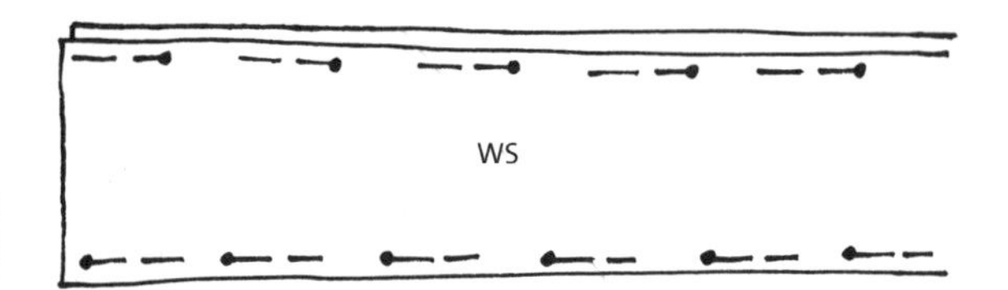


**2** Turn the fabric right side out and carefully press the seams flat to create a neat finish.

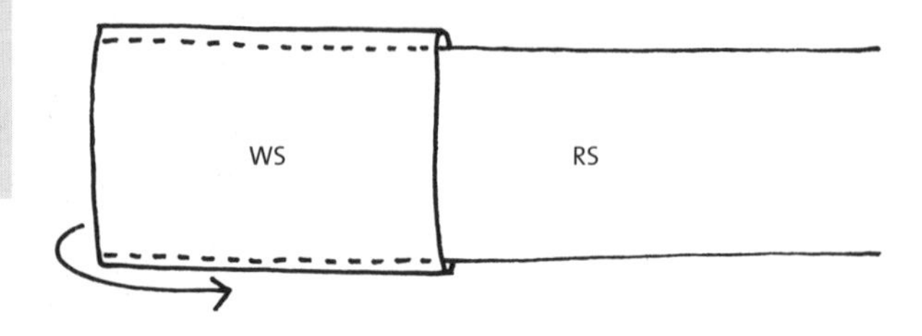


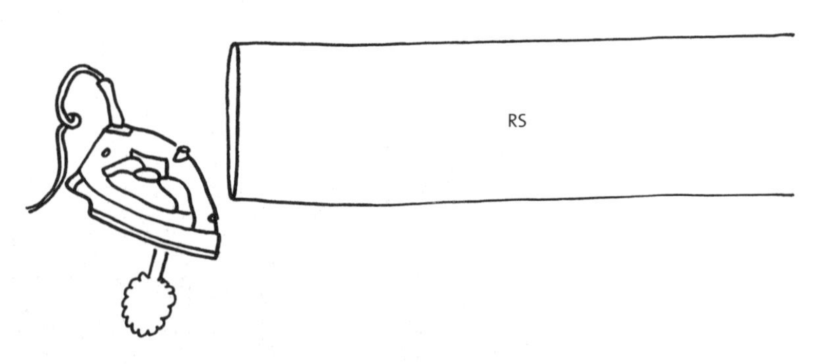

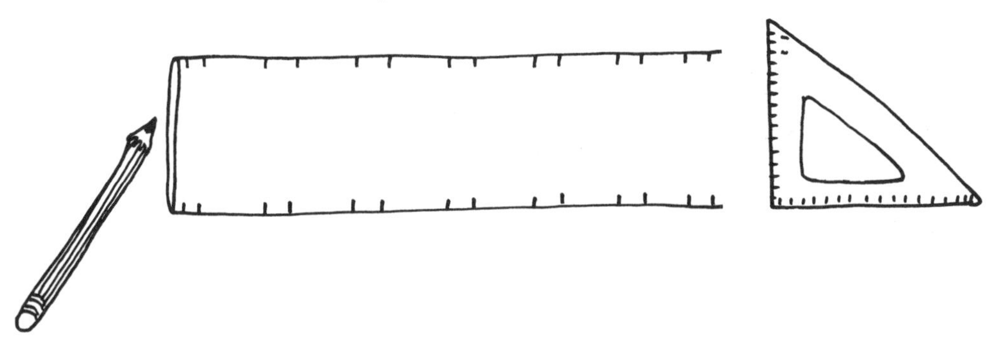

**3** Prepare the box pleats by carefully measuring 5cm (2in) for each box pleat and 3.5cm (1¼in) for each space between the pleats along the length of the rectangle of fabric. Use a set square to ensure that the marks marry up in straight lines.

**4** Fold the box pleats and press into place.

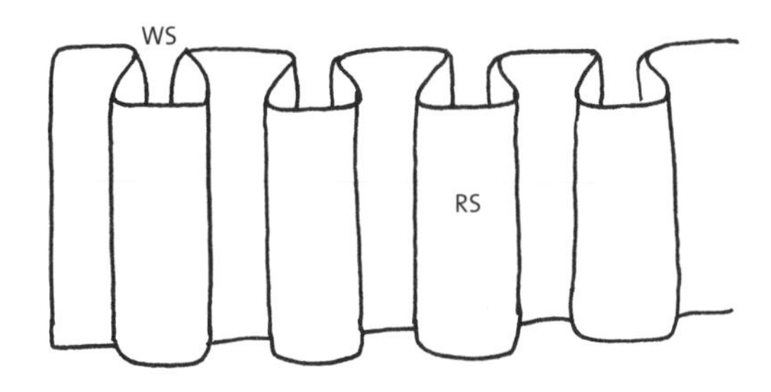


**5** Pin and machine stitch the two space marks together to create each fold. Open up the folds and press them flat to each side of the line of stitching to form the box pleats.

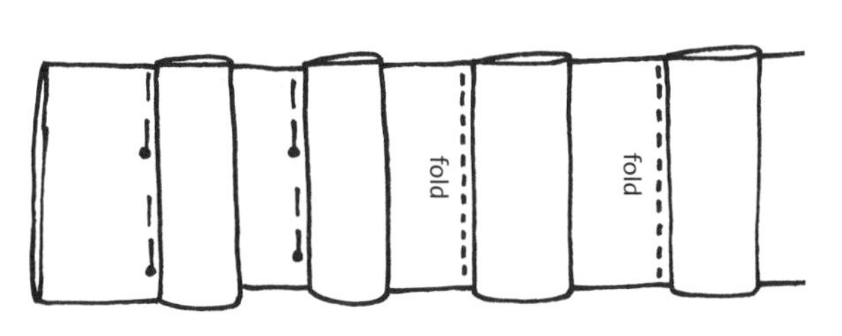


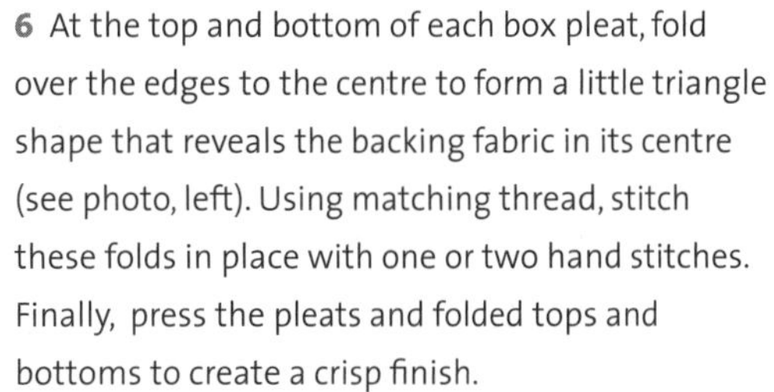

**6** At the top and bottom of each box pleat, fold over the edges to the centre to form a little triangle shape that reveals the backing fabric in its centre (see photo, left). Using matching thread, stitch these folds in place with one or two hand stitches. Finally, press the pleats and folded tops and bottoms to create a crisp finish.

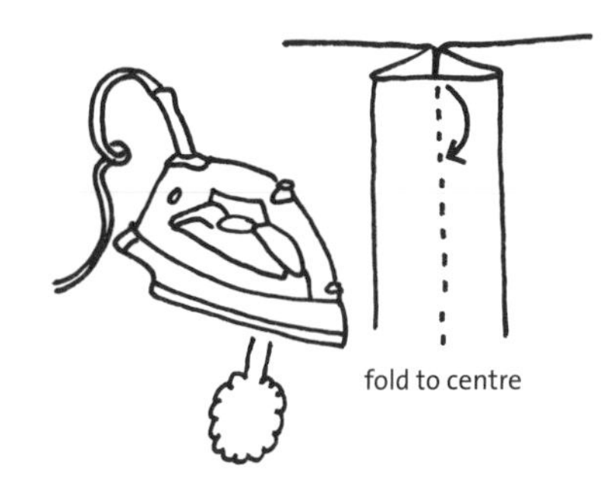


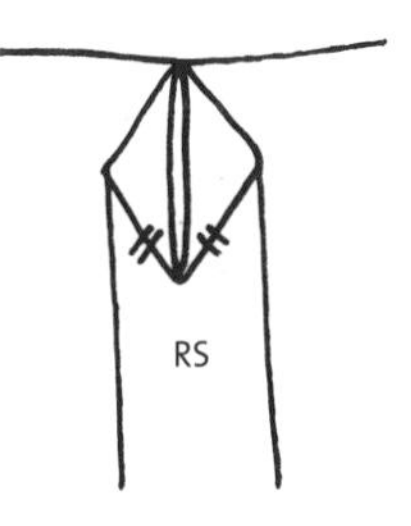


**7** Place the pleated length around your waist and position the belt buckle at each end. Trim the belt to size and fold the belt to fit into the buckle, securing in place on the back of the belt with a few hand stitches.

# pintucking

Pintucks are little folds of fabric that sit on the fabric's surface. They are similar to pleats but much narrower. Pintucks are traditionally arranged in parallel lines and stitched close to one another. They are often used in shirts or blouses to reduce bulk and shape a garment, much in the same way as darts or pleats, while providing a decorative finish.

Pintucking can also be a very creative way to alter the surface of a flat fabric. The effects can be highly sculptural as the fabric can be twisted and manipulated into interesting forms. Fabrics with a natural sheen can offer some unique effects when pintucked, such as an interesting play of light and shade.

Although traditionally pintucks are evenly spaced in regular lines, you can experiment with something less formal. Why not create wavy tucks, criss-crossed tucks or a series of little pintucks with differing spacing between the rows?

Today there are special attachments for sewing machines that can be used to help create pintucks. There is a range of pintuck feet with different-sized grooves on the underside of the foot – the smaller the grooves, the tinier the pintucks will be. These pintuck feet are used together with a twin-sewing needle, which also comes in a range of sizes. The larger the space in between the needles, the larger the tuck will be and vice versa.

You can also use a twin-sewing needle with an ordinary presser foot. But to do so you will need to tighten up the thread tension on the underside of the plate. This is normally achieved by turning a very small screw on the bobbin case. Experiment on a spare piece of fabric to ensure that you are achieving a good result.

◀ These closely spaced rows of tiny pintucks were formed with a special pintuck foot on the sewing machine.

## design samples

Although pintucking is mostly used on plain fabrics, it also produces interesting effects on patterned ones, distorting the pattern in unusual ways. Used primarily for dressmaking, pintucking is also a great technique for runners, throws, cushions and bags, among other things.

First of all, decide what type of fabric you want to use. Finer fabrics work better with this technique than heavier ones as they form smaller folds. If you want a more sculptural effect, choose a fine cotton for example, as it produces crisper little pleats. Whatever your fabric choice, always test your pintuck design first on a spare piece. You can then ensure the settings on the sewing machine are correct before you make your chosen project.

You can also decide whether to use a matching or contrasting thread. Remember there will be two parallel lines of stitching for each tuck, so choose your colour carefully. Do you want it to blend with your fabric or do you want it to make a specific colour statement?

You can opt to make very controlled tucks that are laid out in a strict repetitive manner or you can go for ones that are randomly stitched across the fabric to create a much looser, more expressive look.

The design samples here demonstrate just a few of the ways in which you might use pintucking and a few of the possible fabrics. However, there are no right or wrong methods and you will find it fun to experiment with your own special effects.

A

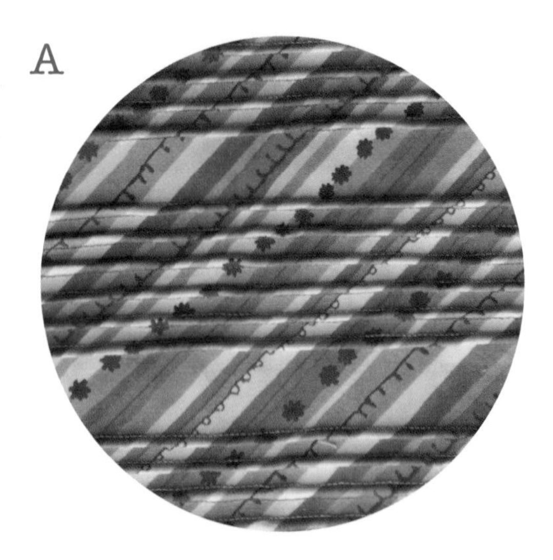

▲ **Sample A:** This sample is created using a vintage cotton fabric with a bold linear print. The pintucking is worked in groups of tiny pleats on the bias of the fabric (at 45 degrees to the selvedge), altering its linear appearance.

B

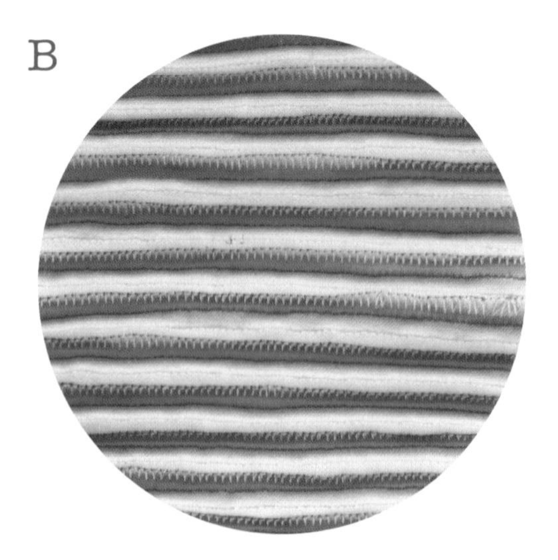

▲ **Sample B:** A beige cotton fabric is pintucked first on the right side of the fabric and then on the wrong side of the fabric, using red sewing thread. The closely spaced pintucking on both sides creates a unique concertina-type fabric that has some elasticity.

C

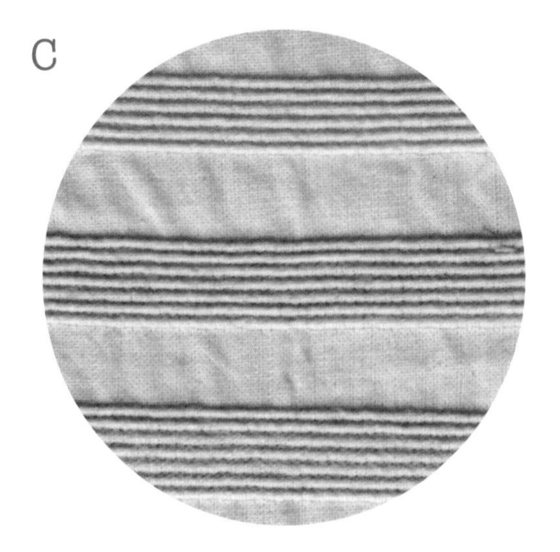

▲ **Sample C:** A plain cream calico is evenly pintucked in regularly spaced groups of very fine pintucks, stitched with matching thread to produce a neat, very formal effect. By positioning the twin-sewing needles close to the previous line of stitching you can create a very closely pintucked fabric.

E

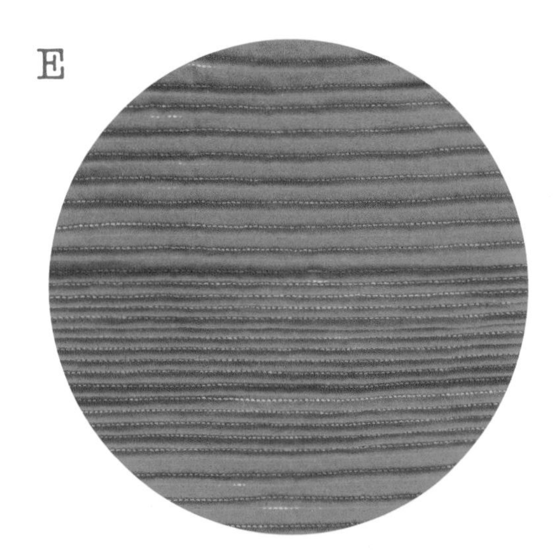

▲ **Sample E:** A plain red cotton fabric is pintucked with the tucks closely set at the centre, and broadening out as they are worked across the fabric. For greater definition, the pintucks are stitched in contrasting blue thread.

D

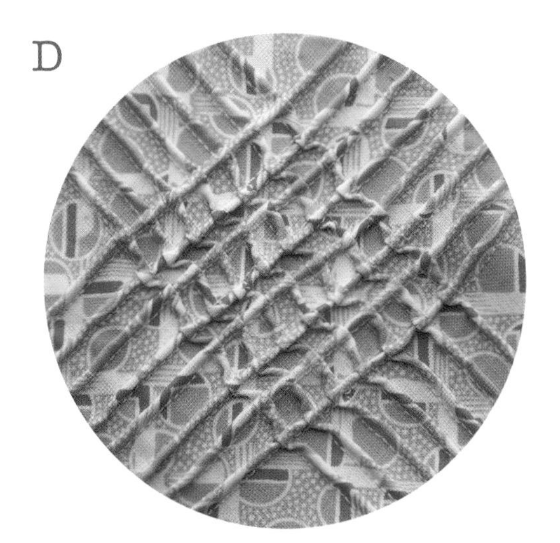

▲ **Sample D:** A vintage printed cotton fabric is pintucked in narrowly spaced groups of pintucks running across the diagonal of the fabric. The first group of pintucks is worked in its entirety before the second group is started.

F

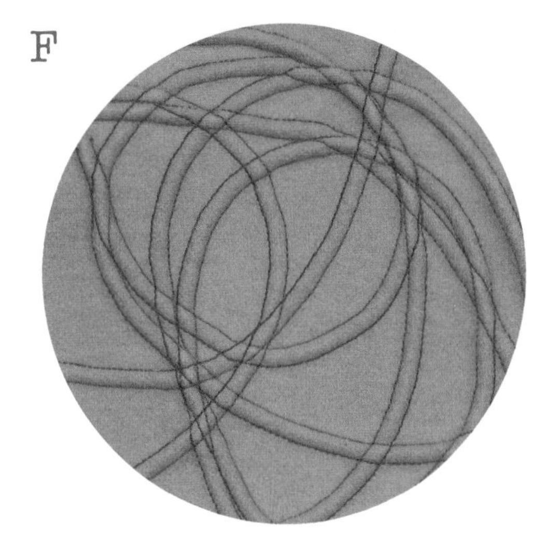

▲ **Sample F:** Here a fine wool fabric is pintucked using two different thread colours in a freeform design. In marked contrast to Sample E, the pintucks here meander and cross each other in an unpredictable manner.

# how to pintuck

Pintucking looks complicated but, in fact, it is very easy to produce professional-looking results.

**Pintuck equipment**

You will need a pintuck foot (**1**) that you can attach to your sewing machine and a twin needle (**2**). Pintuck feet come in a range of sizes: the larger the grooves on the sole of the pintuck foot (**3**), the larger the size of the tucks you will make and, conversely, the smaller the grooves, the smaller the tucks. You will need to choose the correct-sized pintuck needle to accompany the foot you are using. If you do not have a special pintuck foot, you can use a normal presser foot in conjuction with a twin needle, but you will need to adjust the tension to make it tighter, adjusting the small screw on the bobbin (**4**) of your sewing machine.

**Where to stitch pintucks**

Try experimenting with the fabric grain. Sometimes a pintuck will work best if sewn parallel to the selvedge. Or you may find the tucks work better stitched across the weft. Alternatively, see what happens when you sew across the bias (**5**).

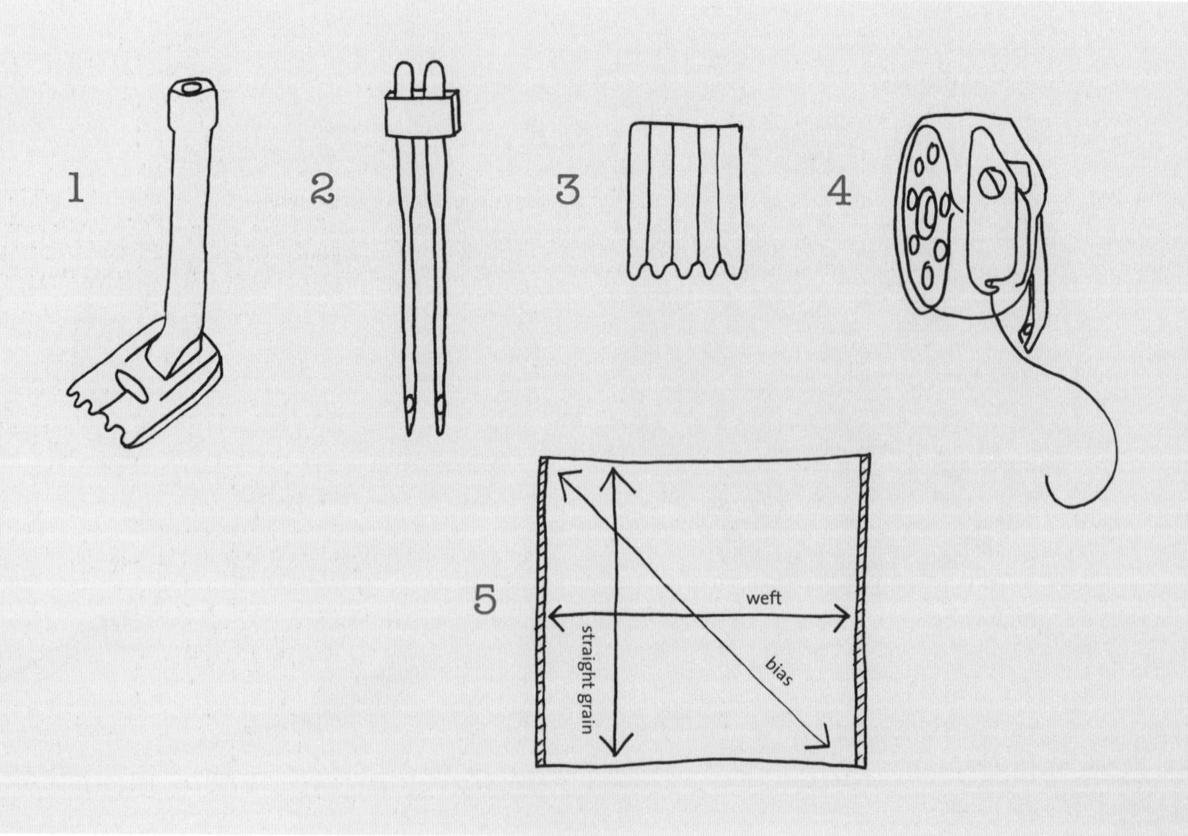

#### Spacing pintucks

Give some thought to spaces in between the tucks as well as their actual width (**6**). Do you want the tucks to be irregularly spaced or have equal spaces between them? For the latter, you can use the presser foot as a guide, as the side of the presser foot is ideal for maintaining equal distance between the tucks.

#### Pintuck experiments

An effective way to strengthen a fine fabric is to criss-cross the pintucks in a grid formation (**7**). Alternatively, try out a linear look or a much more random approach (**8**), letting the pintucks meander across the fabric in a freeform style.

When you create a pintuck on fabric, you are changing the surface from being flat to being three-dimensional. Try altering the visual effect of a pattern's structure on a printed fabric by distorting it with pintucks.

Finally, don't just think about the right side of the fabric. Experiment on the wrong side, too. Try sewing a pintuck on the right side, then flip the fabric over and sew a pintuck on the reverse. If you keep following this order of sewing, the fabric will develop an interesting concertina-like look (**9**), with some elasticity. Using a contrasting sewing thread increases the visual effect.

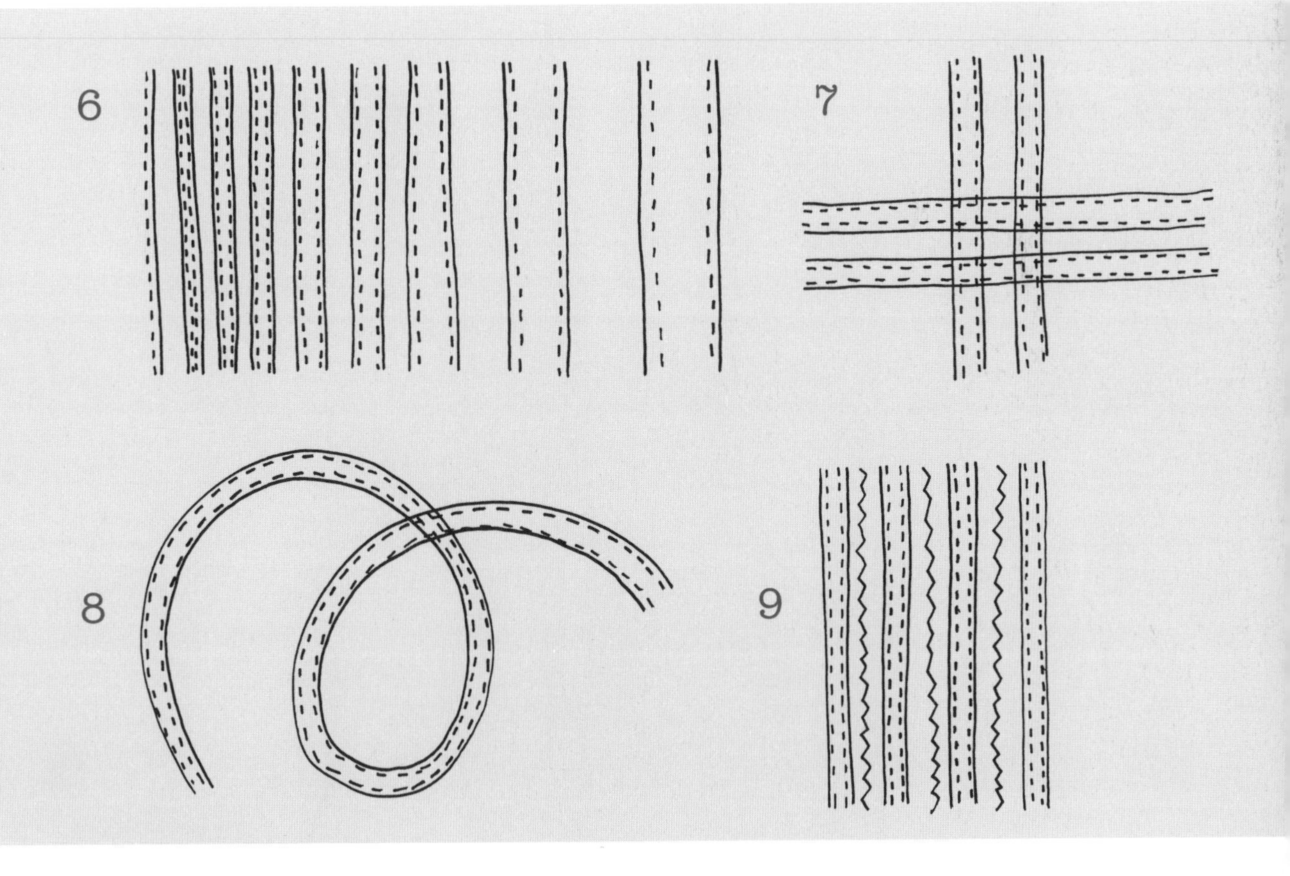

# table runner

Decide on the length and width of the runner. Depending on the size of the pintucks, you will need approximately twice the finished width. The pintucked part of the runner shown measures 90 x 30cm (36 x 12in), plus two patterned borders at each end, each 15cm (6in) deep.

**What you need**

0.5m (½yd) plain cotton fabric; 0.5m (½yd) plain cotton backing fabric; 0.25m (¼yd) patterned cotton fabric; fabric-marking pencil; matching and contrasting thread.

**Making the runner**

**1** Cut out your runner to twice the required width plus the length, with 1.5cm (½in) seam allowance all around. Mark the centre of the width. Work the pintucks from the centre out to one side, using contrasting thread. On the runner shown all the pintucks are set close together with 15 pintucks in the centre, 8 spaced slightly wider apart and 6 with more space again. Repeat for the other side.

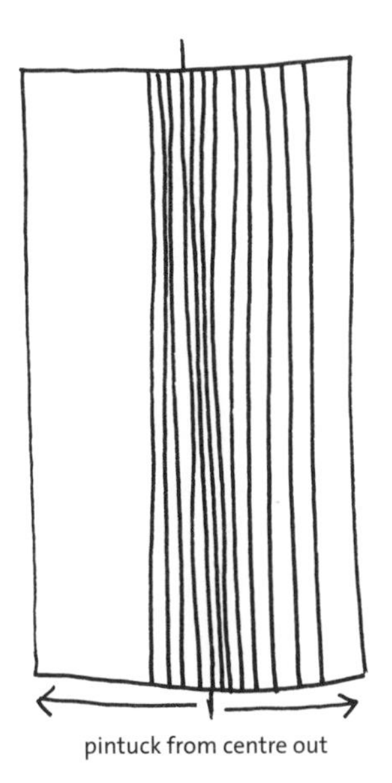


**2** Trim excess fabric, leaving a 1.5cm (½in) seam allowance at each side. Press the pintucks in one direction.

**3** For the backing, cut a length of plain cotton fabric to match the size of the pintucked piece. Place both fabrics right sides together and machine stitch the two long sides with a 1.5cm (½in) seam allowance, using a straight stitch. Press the seams open and turn the runner right sides out.

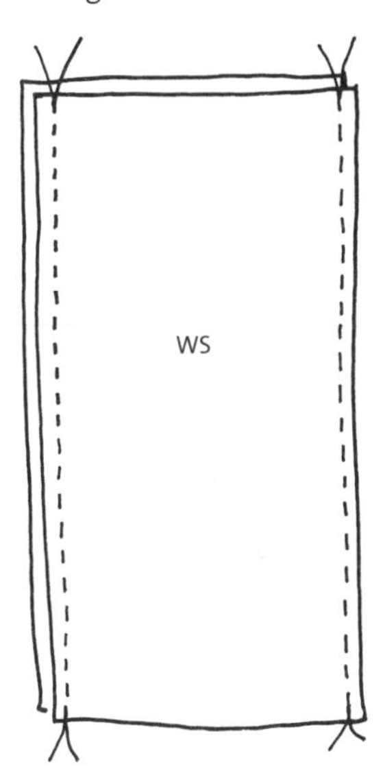


**4** Cut out two pieces of patterned fabric for the borders to the width of the pintucked piece and a depth of 15cm (6in), plus 1.5cm (½in) seam allowance all around. Cut out two pieces of the plain cotton in the same size for the border lining.

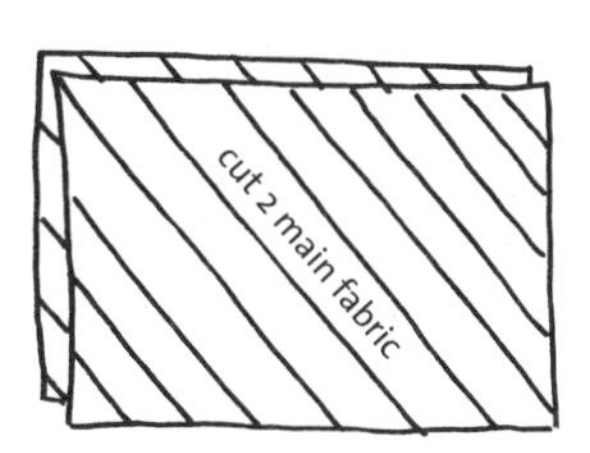


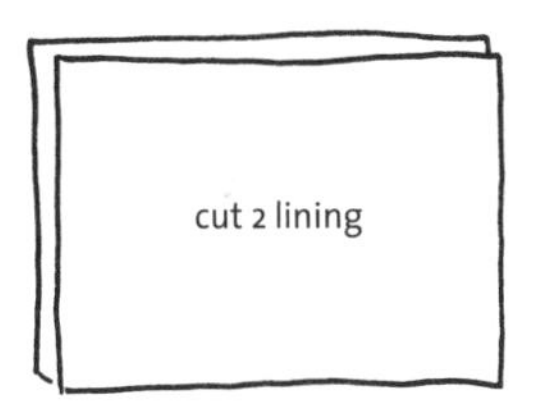

**5** With right sides facing, place one piece of patterned border fabric and one piece of lining together. Sew a straight line down the two short sides and one long side. Clip the corners and press open the seams. Repeat for the other border piece. Turn right sides out.

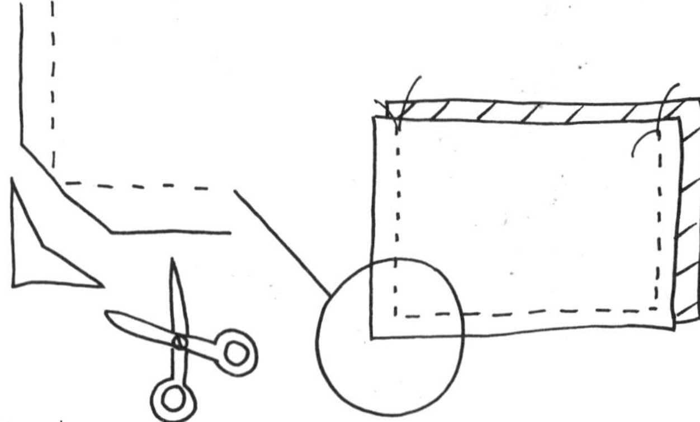

**6** With the right sides facing, place the raw edges of a border piece and the pintucked piece together. Stitch with a seam allowance of 1.5cm (½in). Press the seam open using a steam iron. Repeat for the other border piece.

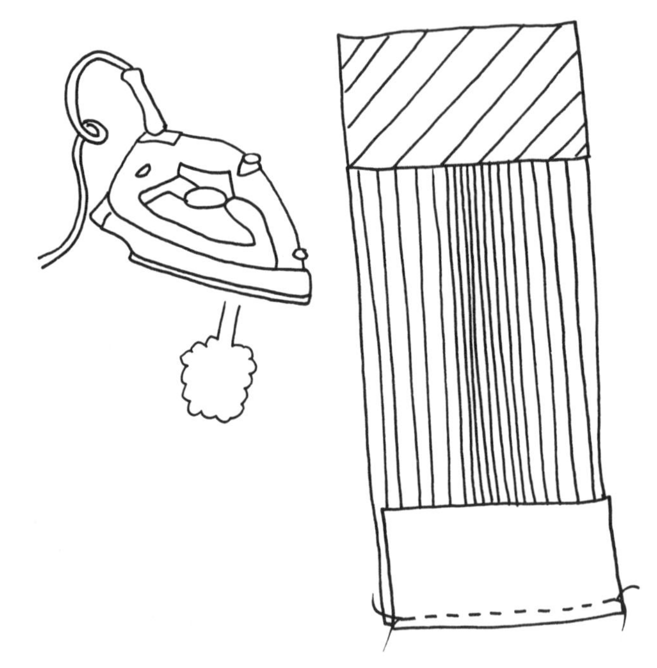

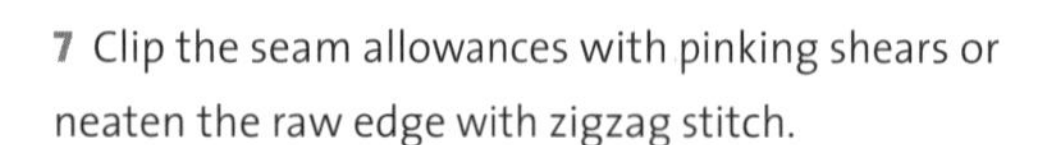

**7** Clip the seam allowances with pinking shears or neaten the raw edge with zigzag stitch.

**To make the tassels**

**8** Rip surplus patterned fabric into six strips 24cm (9½in) long and 2cm (¾in) wide. Use a zigzag stitch to create a cord from each strip (see page 88). Bundle the corded strips together and tie in a double knot in the centre. Fold in half to make a tassel. Repeat to make a tassel for each corner.

**9** Using matching sewing thread, hand stitch a tassel at each corner of the runner.

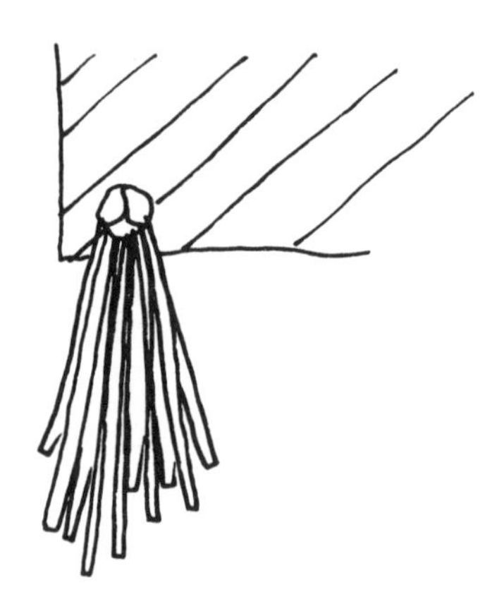

# bag

Decide on the size of your bag. This bag measures 40 x 34.5cm (15¾ x 13½in). If you plan to follow the pintuck design here, then double this size widthways plus half as much again lengthways to determine the amount of fabric for pintucking. For a design with more tucks, remember to allow extra fabric and make a sample to assess how much fabric your pintucks require. The handles are made from strips of the main bag fabric.

**What you need**

0.5m (½yd) printed cotton fabric for the bag and bag handles; 0.5m (½yd) plain cotton fabric for the bag back; 0.25m (¼yd) contrasting cotton fabric for the lining; fabric-marking pencil; matching sewing thread.

**Making the bag**

**1** Cut out the printed cotton to twice the bag width and one and a half times the depth required. Mark the positions for all the groups of pintucks: approximately one third of the way up from the bottom for the horizontal tucks and evenly spaced across the width for the vertical tucks.

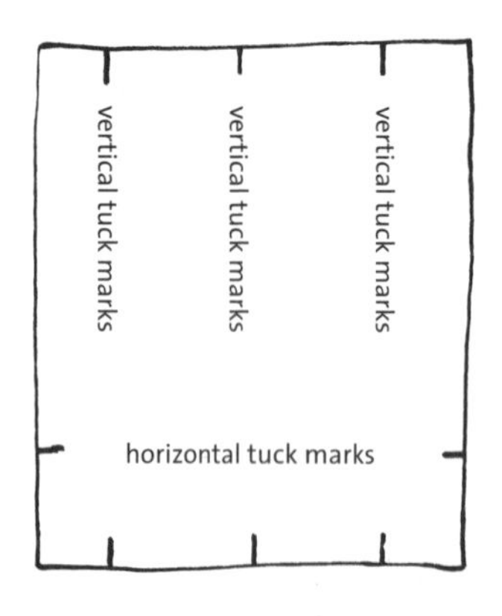


**2** Stitch the first of each group of pintucks (see page 58) to set the positions. Use either matching or contrasting thread.

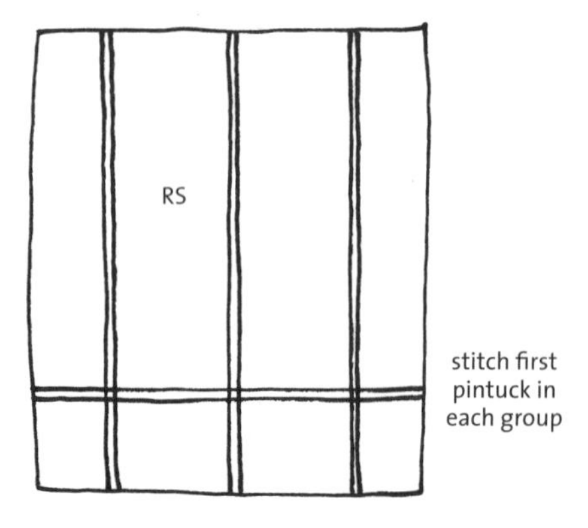


**3** Then complete all the pintuck groups as required, so that you have groups of five, seven and five vertical pintucks and one group of eight horizontal pintucks.

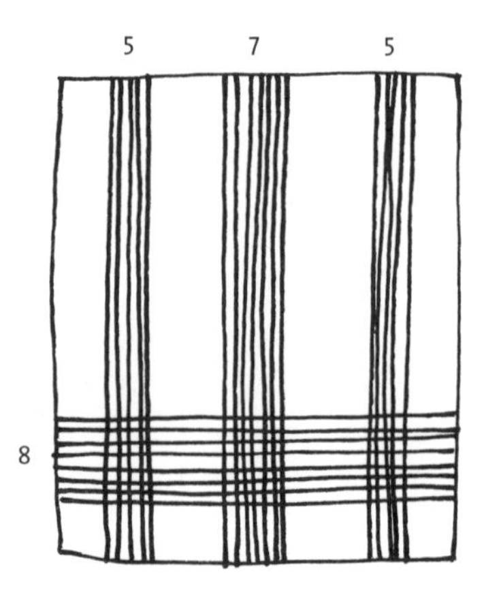

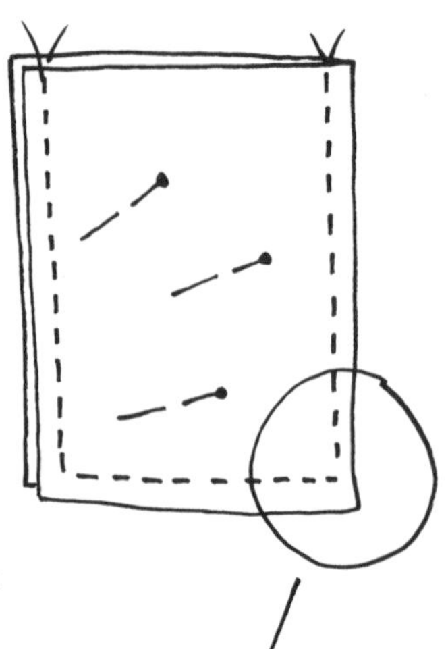

**4** Cut away the surplus fabric from the bag front, leaving a 1.5cm (½in) seam allowance. Cut a piece of back fabric to match the size of the front.

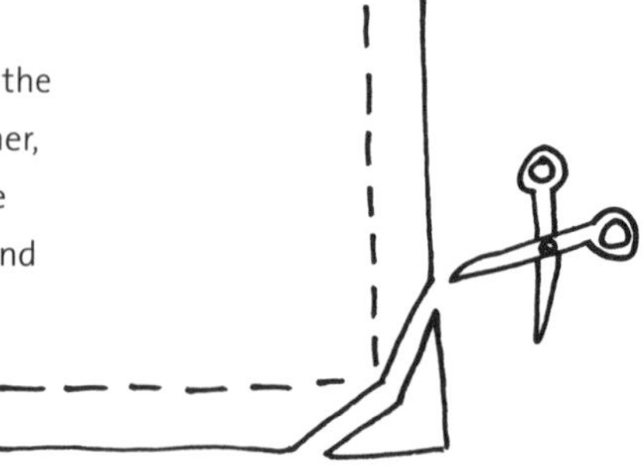

**5** With the front and back of the bag placed right sides together, stitch the side seams and the base. Clip away the corners and press open the seams.

**Making the lining**

**6** Create a lining for the bag using two pieces of lining fabric cut to the size indicated in Step 4 and stitch as Step 5.

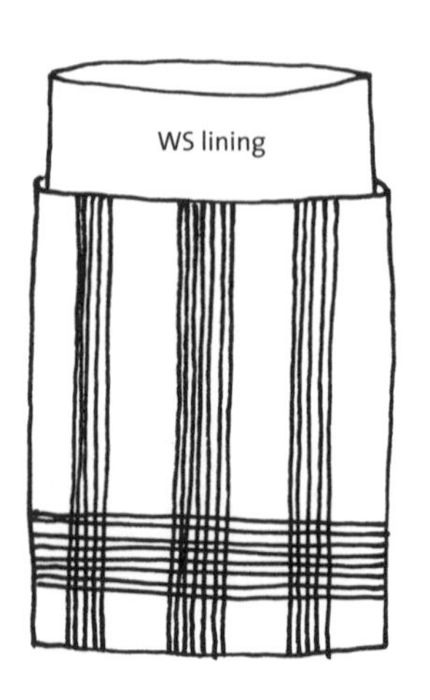


**7** With wrong sides together, slip the lining inside the bag.

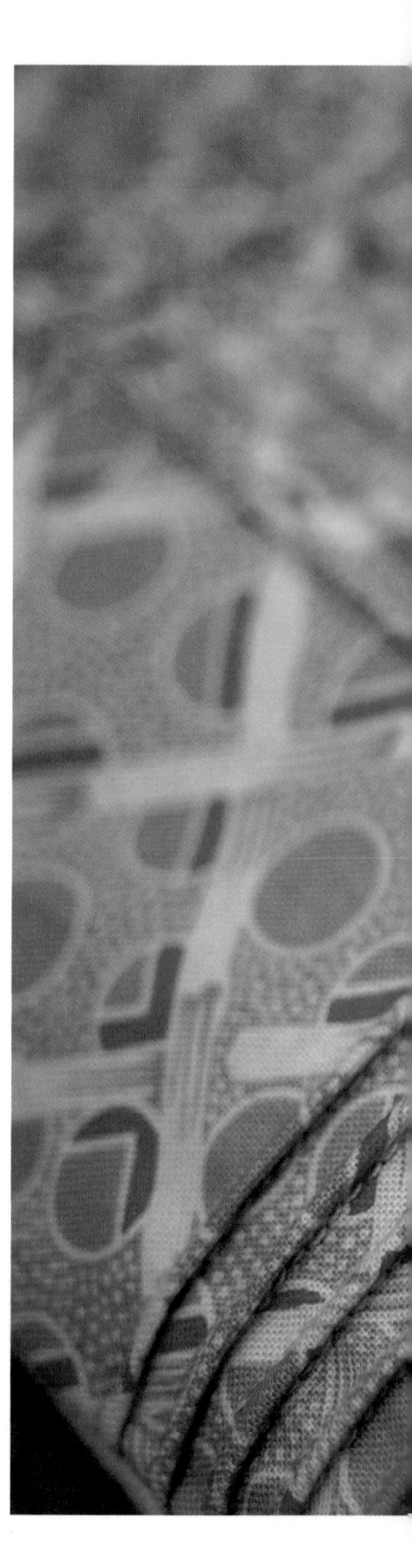

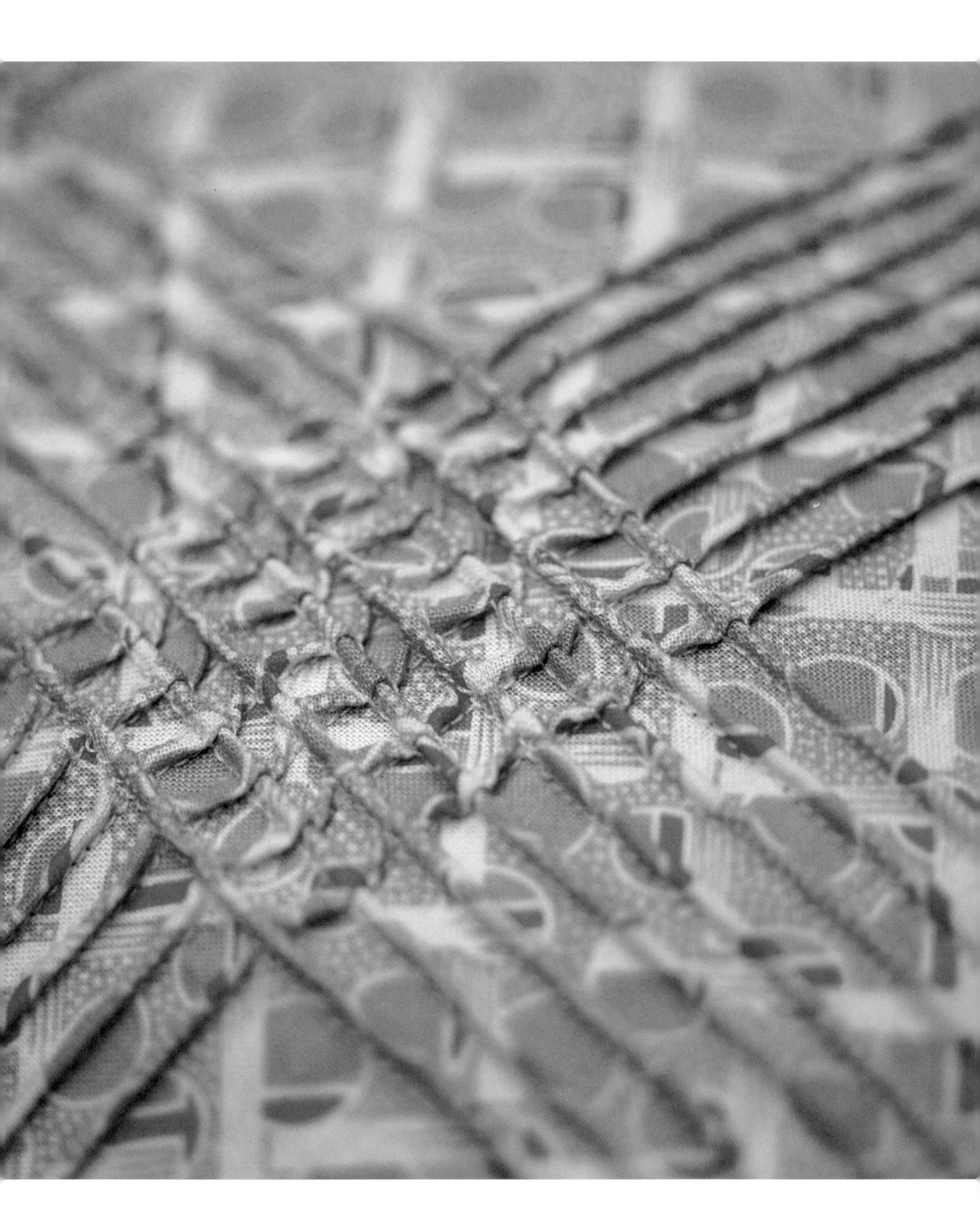

**Making the handles**

**8** Rip the bag fabric into eight strips measuring 6cm (2½in) wide, each 15cm (6in) long, plus one additional strip of fabric 10cm (4in) wide and 30cm (12in) long.

**9** Pin the long strip to a table to secure for the handle base. Starting at one end of the bundle of strips, knot these around the wider strip using overhand knots. Continue knotting the bundle until it covers the length of the large strip of fabric. (The artwork treats the bundles as one strip.) Repeat Steps 8 and 9 for the other handle.

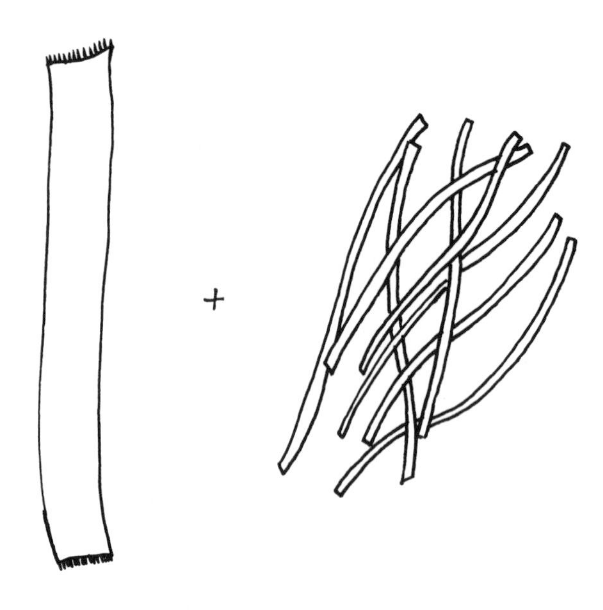


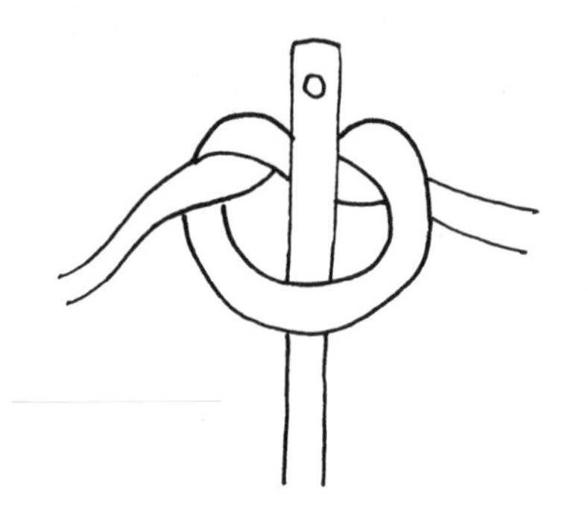

knot strip around base strip

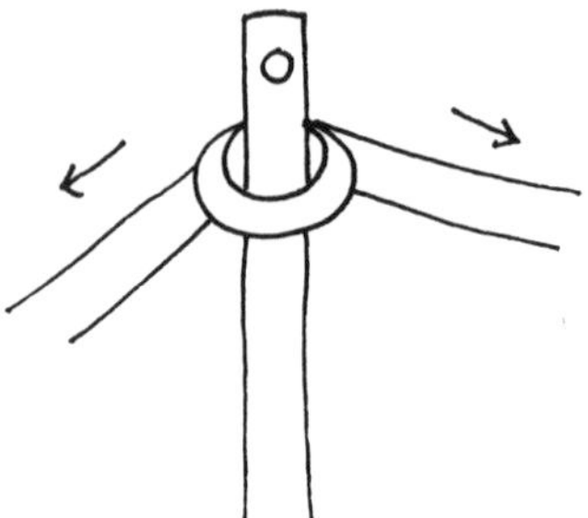

pull tight

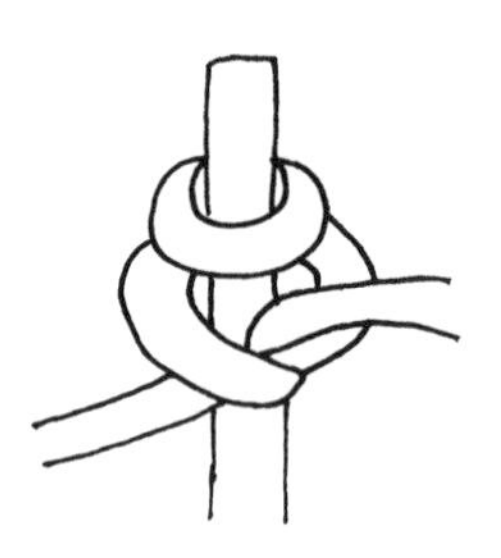

knot again

repeat as needed

**Finishing the bag**

**10** Fold 1.5cm (½in) of the top edge of the bag to the inside and press flat. Then fold over the lining of the bag to the outside so it just extends over the top of the bag. Press flat.

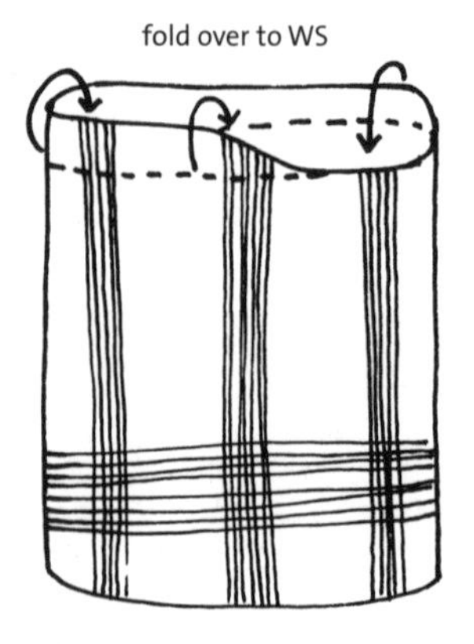


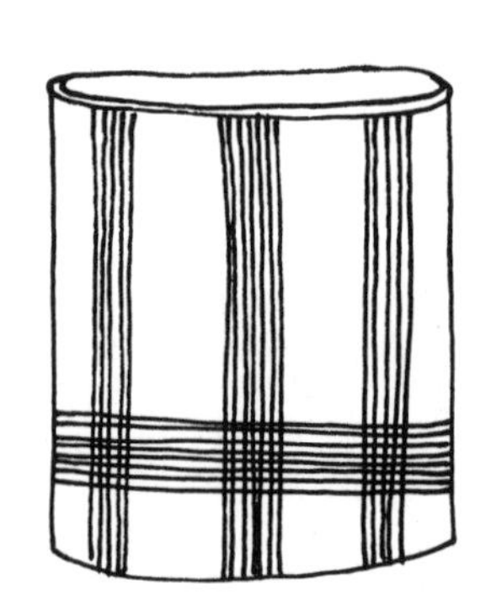

**11** Position one handle on the front of the bag, sliding it down so that the ends fit between the outer bag and the lining. Check the size and trim off any surplus ends. Pin in place. Match the other handle to the position and length of the first, and pin in place. Topstitch the top of the bag to secure the handles and lining.

**12** For a decorative touch, tie some cords (see page 88) around the handle. Press the bag lightly.

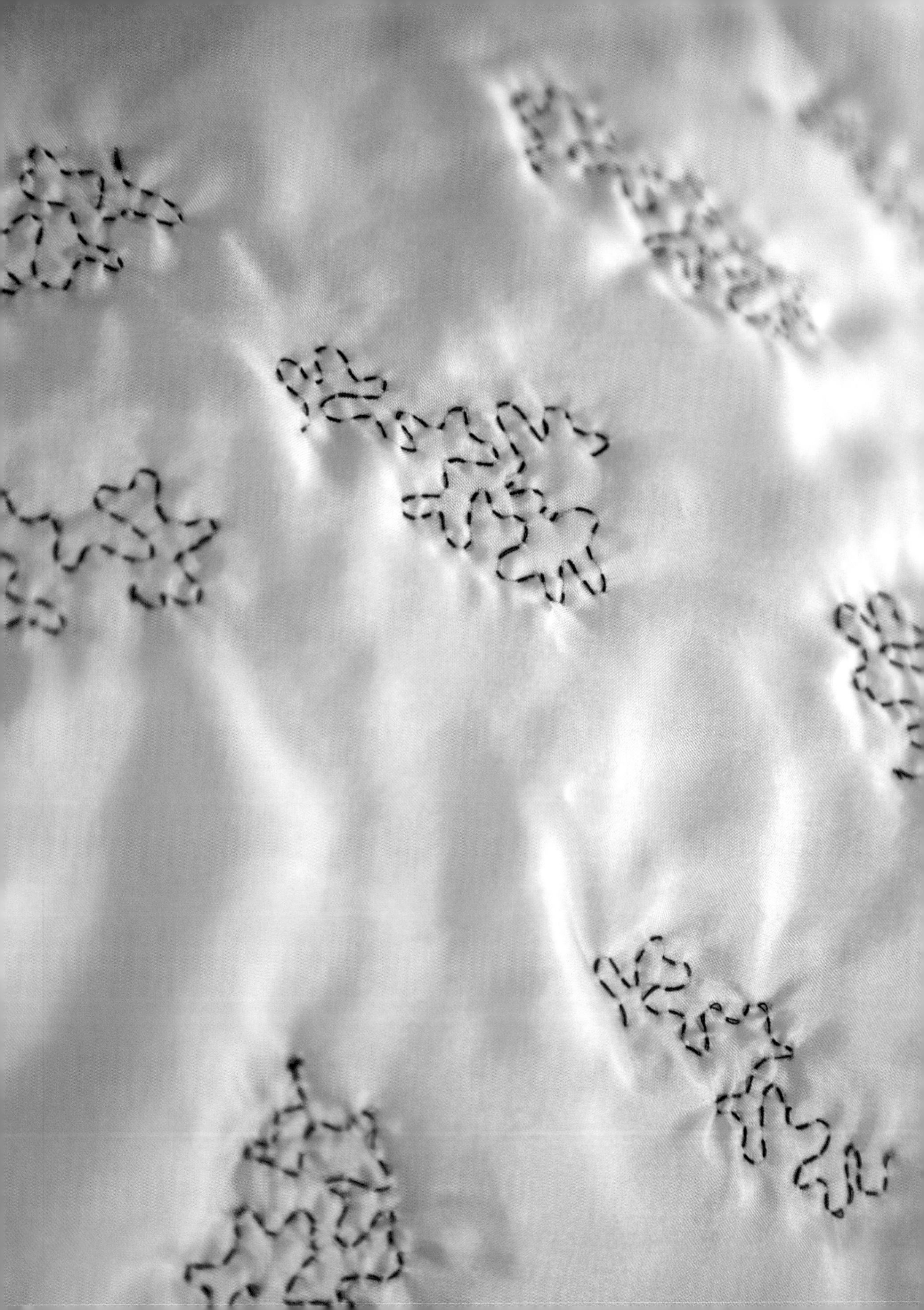

# quilting

Quilting is a technique that has been around for many hundreds of years. In it a number of layers of fabric are stitched together primarily for warmth – mostly for garments or blankets. It has subsequently become highly decorative but with the added value of comfort, too.

Quilting is a versatile technique. You can use both hand stitching and machine stitching to combine the layers of fabric in practical and decorative ways. Try combining hand stitching with machine stitching, and see what inventive ideas you can come up with.

Your quilted projects can be thick or thin. There is a wide variety of different waddings on the market. Although many are man-made and provide a very robust and firm fabric, there are also traditional waddings in cotton or wool, which give a flatter and firmer result. You can pull the wadding apart for thinner layers or even add extra layers, and you can create regular or freeform quilting patterns. Remember the thicker the wadding, the more pronounced the quilted effect will be. The less wadding used, the softer and more delicate the effect.

When choosing the form of the quilting, it pays to experiment first. Try different types of wadding to check the effect they produce and experiment with different types and thicknesses of thread for the quilt stitches.

In addition, the type of thread used and the type of stitching – hand or machine – that binds the fabrics together has a great bearing on the final appearance of the piece, as well as how long it will take to complete. Generally, hand-quilted items take more time and care, and look more precious.

◀ Fine cream silk has been quilted in tiny swirls using hand stitches in black sewing thread, inspired by the printed fabric in Sample B on page 73.

# design samples

There are many purposes for quilted items. Practical items like quilts, cot blankets, bed covers and smaller items, such as tea cosies, cafetière covers and computer cases, can all benefit from the warmth and cushioning of quilted layers of fabric.

Experiment with the 3-D nature of quilting by trying out different types of fabric with different types of wadding and with different styles of stitching to hold them together.

The quilting stitches will be a major feature of the design, so experiment with both machine and hand stitches. You can also use different thicknesses of yarn or thread for the hand stitches, creating little knotted tufts, perhaps, or, as I have done here in Samples C and F, you can add small decorative pieces of fabric to mark the tufts, rather like the tufting on a traditional mattress.

Although quilting is usually very symmetrical, it does not have to be so. You can make your designs more interesting by quilting over parts of a printed fabric (as in Sample B) in a contrasting colour. Or you can patch the fabrics together but then make the patches up so that they are slightly irregular. Try turning one patch slightly (as in Sample E) to draw attention to it.

Draw your inspiration from these design samples, perhaps mixing the ideas together to come up with your own alternatives.

A

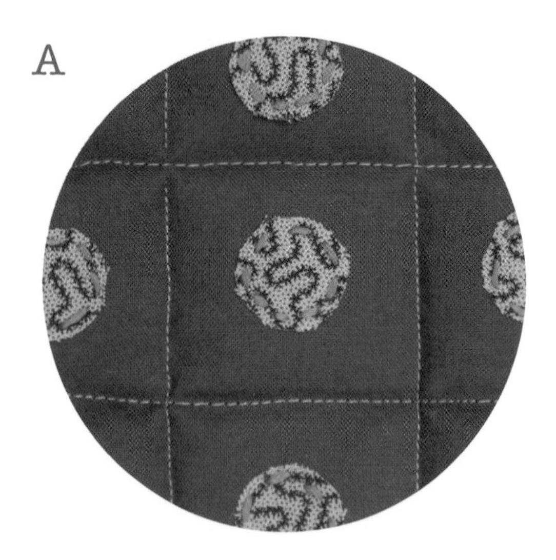

▲ **Sample A:** The fabric has been marked and stitched into squares. The patterned fabric in Sample B has been cut into small circles, placed in each square, and outlined with a few contrasting orange running stitches. The piece is then machine quilted through all layers along the outlines of the squares.

B

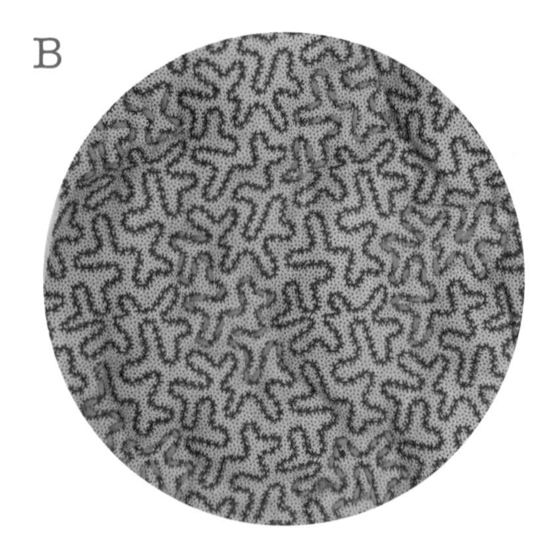

▲ **Sample B:** Here, parts of the pattern on a printed cotton fabric are quilted through all layers by outlining them in small running stitches in contrasting thread.

C

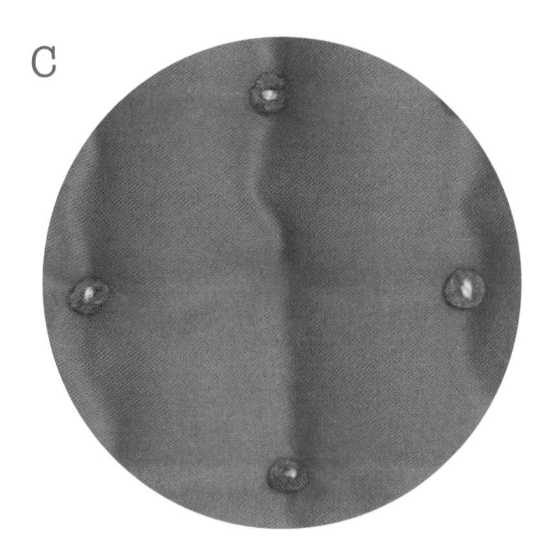

▲ **Sample C:** In this sample, tiny circles are cut from felt with a hole punch. These circles are then positioned in a grid-like desgin on the red base fabric and hand quilted through all the layers using contrasting sewing thread.

D

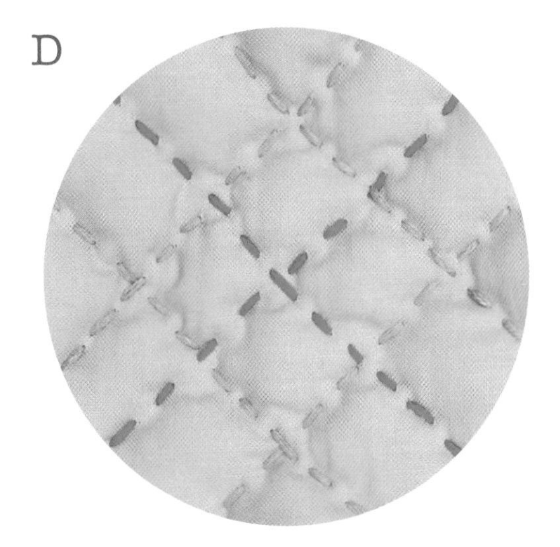

▲ **Sample D:** Here, a plain cotton has been hand-quilted in diagonal rows to create a diamond pattern, using two colours of six-stranded embroidery thread and a simple running stitch through all the layers.

E

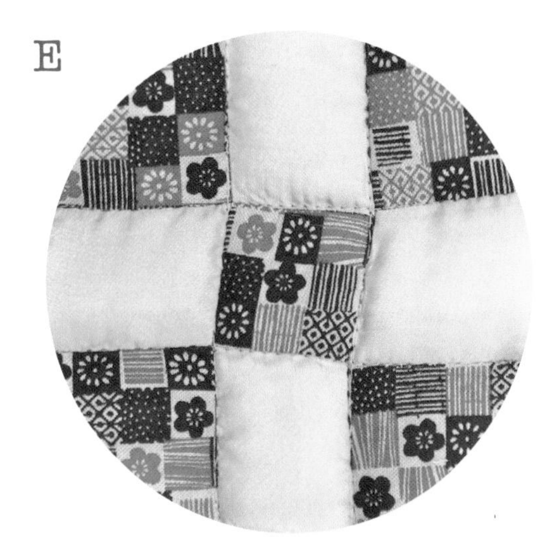

▲ **Sample E:** In this sample, squares of roughly equal sizes are cut from plain cream silk and a printed cotton. The squares, which are purposely slightly irregular, are first patched together, then the patchwork piece is layered with wadding and backing fabric and quilted by machine, using the squares as a stitching guide.

F

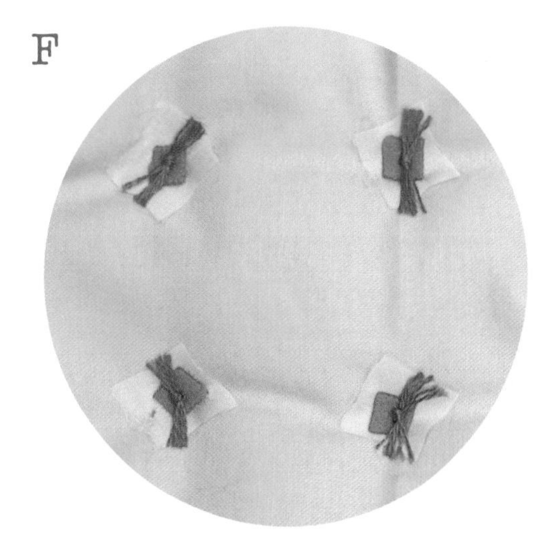

▲ **Sample F:** This sample is a variation on Sample C. Here, small squares of silk and felt have been cut and placed on top of each other in a regular grid formation on the surface of the fabric. Stranded cotton is used to hand tuft all the layers together.

# how to quilt

Before you quilt you need to sandwich a layer of wadding between two pieces of fabric. Do this neatly so that your quilting looks professional and the fabrics stay firmly together throughout the stitching process.

**Quilting techniques**

Cut out two identical-sized pieces of fabric, one for the front and one for the back. Then cut a piece of wadding to the same measurement.

Sandwich the wadding in between the two pieces of fabric (**1**), with wrong sides facing the wadding. You can peel thick wadding apart into thinner layers if necessary.

Pin the three layers together at intervals. Tack the layers of fabric together using large stitches across the fabric at a 45-degree angle. Continue in evenly spaced lines until the fabric is covered. Repeat, working in the opposite direction (**2**) to secure the sandwiched layers.

Your fabric is now ready for quilting either by machine or hand stitching. Once the layers are permanently quilted, you can carefully remove the tacking stitches.

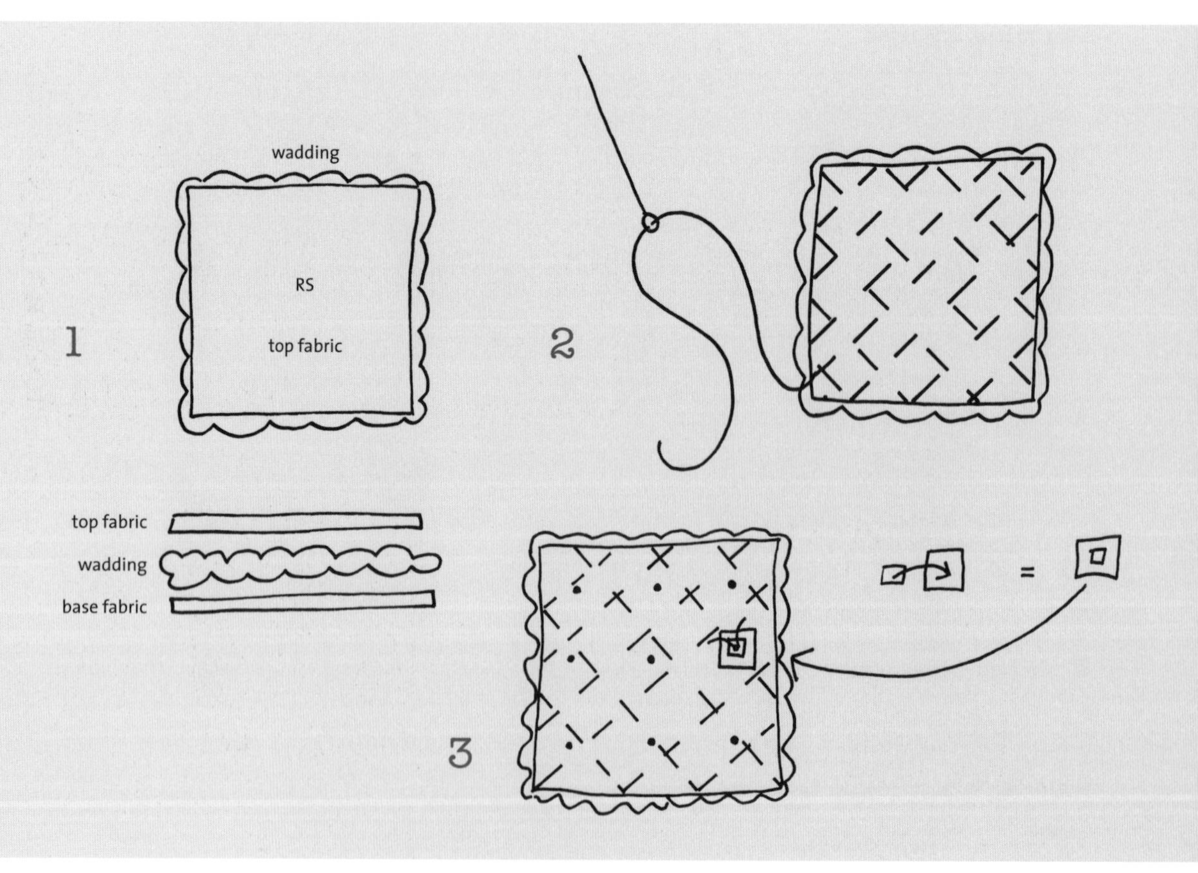

**Quilting effects**

You can choose to hand stitch or machine stitch your quilted design. Whatever method you use, the stitches have to go through all three layers of the fabric. Hand stitching is particularly good when creating decorative effects. For example, you can cut little squares (1.5cm/½in square) and then cut smaller squares to sit on top. The squares are laid on top of each other and hand stitched through the prepared layers of fabric using a six-stranded cotton. This is stitched through and tied off on the top so that the knot is visible (**3**). The same idea can be used with different shapes, such as the circles in Sample C on page 73.

Patchwork pieces provide an ideal base for machine quilting, with quilting stitches following the outline of the patchwork shapes. For a simple patchwork effect, cut fabric into squares. Join the squares together to form a strip (**4a**). Press the seams flat. Sew the strips together to create a block (**4b**). When you have created a block to the correct dimensions for your quilted piece, cut wadding and a base fabric to the same size and tack together. You can quilt by topstitching around each square (**4c**) or patchwork shape, or incorporating other quilting effects with hand or machine stitches.

For a looser more organic effect, quilt in spirals or swirls, perhaps following only part of the pattern either by hand (**5**), as in the egg cosies on page 80, or by machine.

Alternatively, cut out circles or shapes from a contrasting fabric, hand stitch in place on the prepared quilt before machine sewing straight lines across the fabric (**6**) – see also Sample A, page 72.

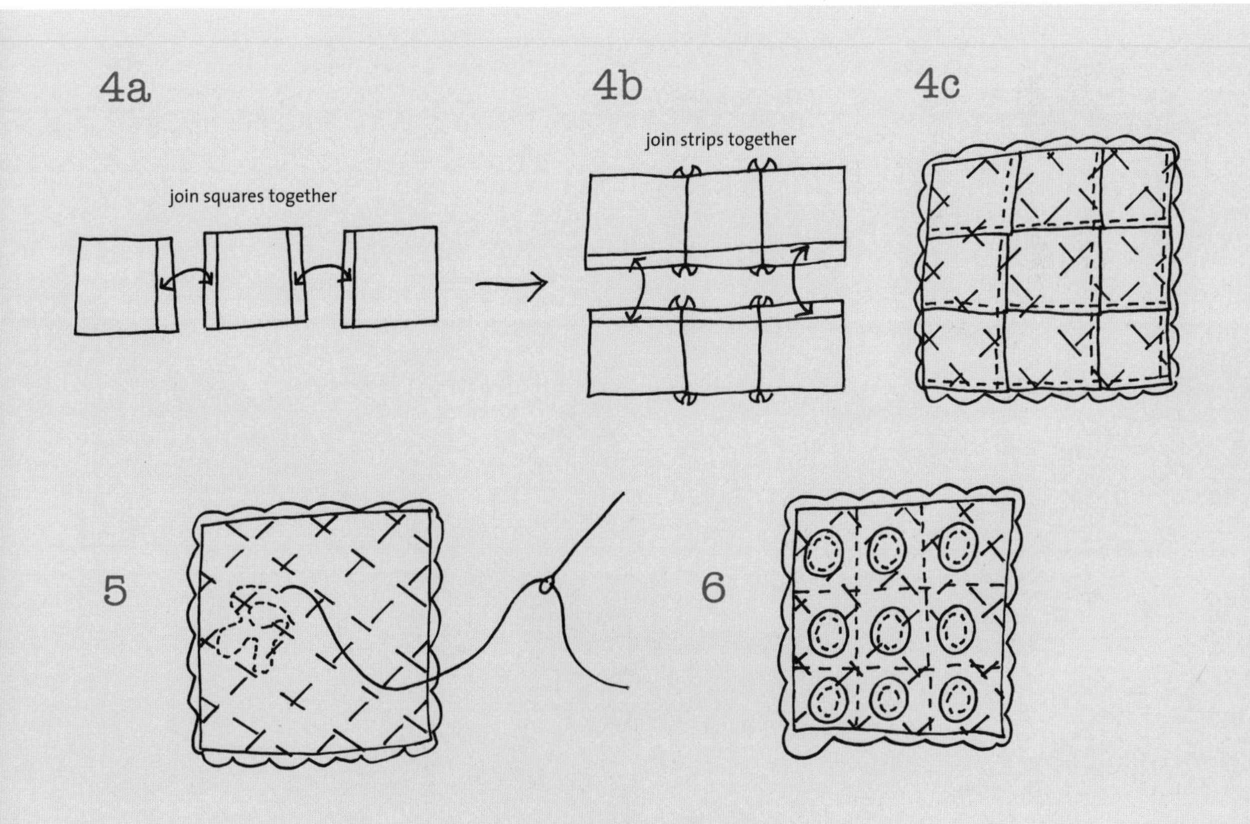

# chair pad

You can make several chair pads, perhaps in matching but not identical fabrics, using three colours, as shown here, but varying the top fabric. Because the pads are small, it does not take long to hand quilt them. The cords that are used to tie them to the chair are shown on page 88. The chair pad shown measures 30cm (12in) square.

**What you need**

Enough cotton fabric to make a pad of the right size (front and back), measure the area of the chair to be covered, add 4cm (1½in) all around for seam allowances and to allow for the fabric reducing in the quilting process; contrasting cotton for the base of the pad; wadding; small amount of silk and felt fabric for squares; fabric-marking pencil; contrasting six-stranded embroidery thread; two cords from base cotton fabric, about 70cm (28in) long (see page 88).

**Preparing the fabric layers**

**1** Cut out two pieces of fabric to the measurements required, one for the top and one for the back of the quilted piece. Cut another piece of contrasting cotton for the base of the pad.

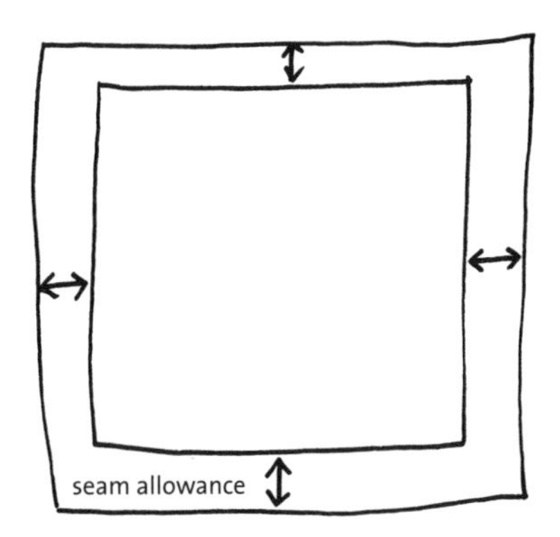


**2** Cut the wadding to the finished size of the pad. Sandwich the top and back fabric and wadding together and pin layers together.

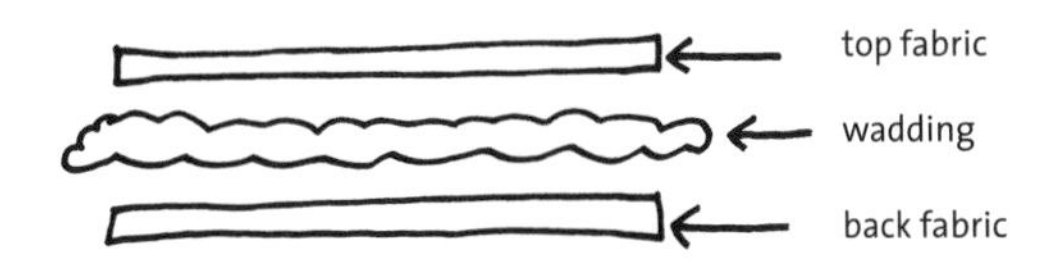


**3** Tack the pieces together (see page 74).

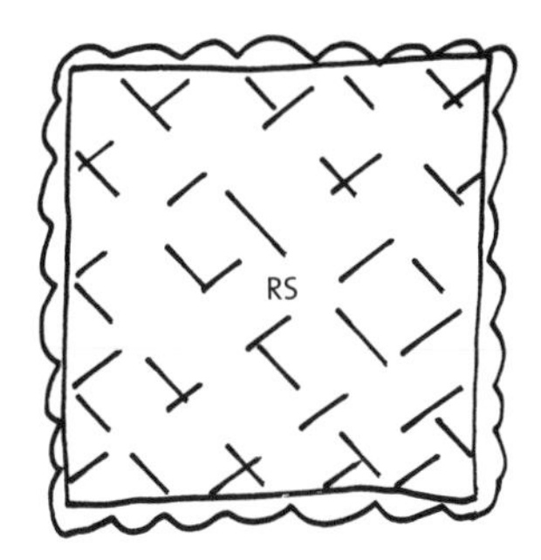


**4** On the right side of the top fabric, mark out the positions for the rows of tiny squares with a fabric-marking pencil. Cut out sufficient pairs of squares of silk and felt, one slightly larger than the other. The felt squares shown are 7mm (3/8in) square; the silk squares shown are 1.5cm (½in) square.

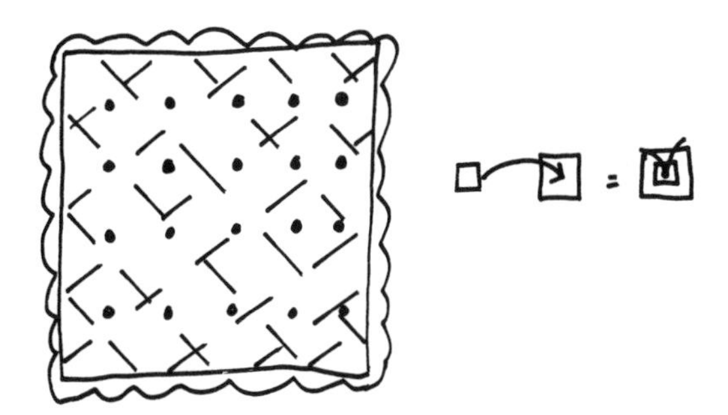

**5** Position the pairs of squares, tying them through the layers with contrasting embroidery thread and knotting the ends (see below). Make sure that you work through the three layers to give the maximum quilted effect.

**6** To finish the chair pad, lay the quilted piece right side down on the right side of the backing fabric. Fold the prepared ties or cords in half and pin in place on one side of the cushion pad, leaving 5cm (2in) of the folded end showing. Taking a 1.5cm (½in) seam allowance, and with the sewing machine set to a straight stitch, line up the edge of the foot with the edge of the quilted area and sew around the pad, leaving the area between the pair of ties unstitched for turning through.

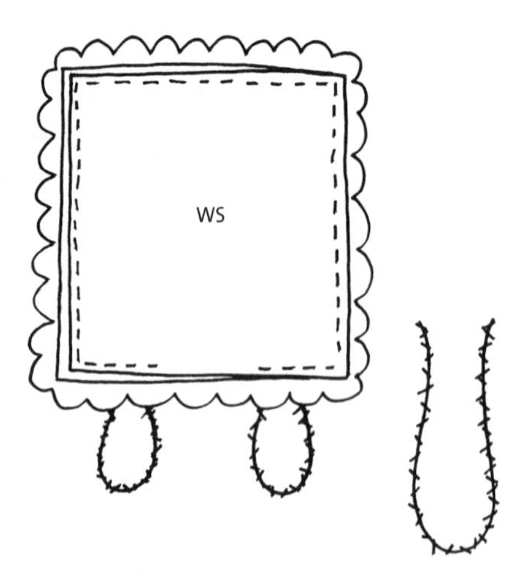


**7** Trim any excess fabric and wadding. Turn the pad right sides out, and slip stitch the gap closed. Tie the cushion to the chair.

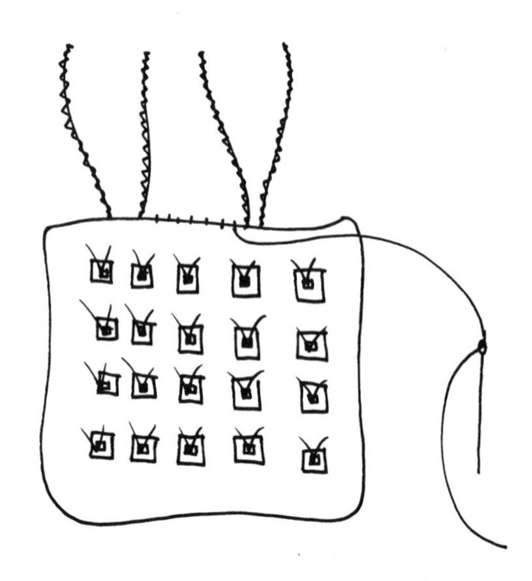

### ● ● ● KNOTTED TUFTS

You can make simple knotted tufts to quilt layers of fabric together. Using a suitable-sized sewing needle and thread, stitch through the layers of fabric, starting on the top layer of fabric, leaving a long thread on the top layer (about 10cm/4in long). Bring the threads back up to the top again. Repeat this if needed. Then knot the threads on the top layer with a double knot before trimming off.

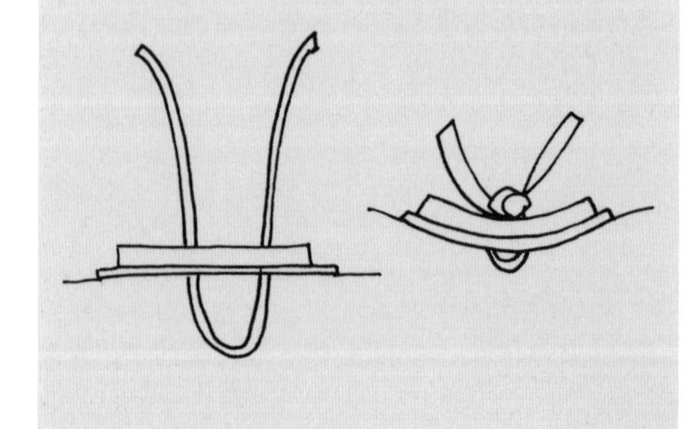

# egg cosies

The patterned fabric for these little cosies has an elegant, Japanese look. Choose a contrasting colour embroidery thread to allow the decorative hand stitching to show. You can vary the fabrics and the quilting effects for a set of cosies. Try criss-crossed lines of running stitches in a contrasting colour on a plain fabric (as on page 82), making sure the stitches go through all the layers. The cosies shown measure 11 x 8cm (4½ x 3¼in).

**What you need**

Small piece of patterned cotton fabric for front; small piece of plain cotton for back and lining; wadding; narrow contrasting ribbon for loop; contrasting six-stranded embroidery thread; embroidery needle.

**Making the cosy**

**1** Measure the height and width of your egg cup (with an egg in it). Draw a rectangle to this measurement on paper, adding 1.5cm (½in) seam allowances. Mark the centre on the width. Fold the rectangle in half lengthwise. Draw a curve joining the top and halfway marks. Cut out the template.

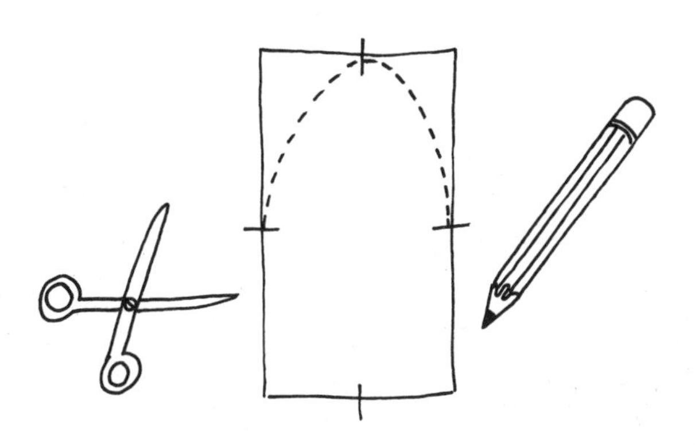

**2** Using the template, cut out four fabric pieces (one patterned and one plain for the front and two plain for the back) and two wadding pieces.

**3** Sandwich the wadding between the two pieces of fabric for the front and back of the egg cosy, creating two layered pieces. Tack the layers together but do not stitch the two sides together yet.

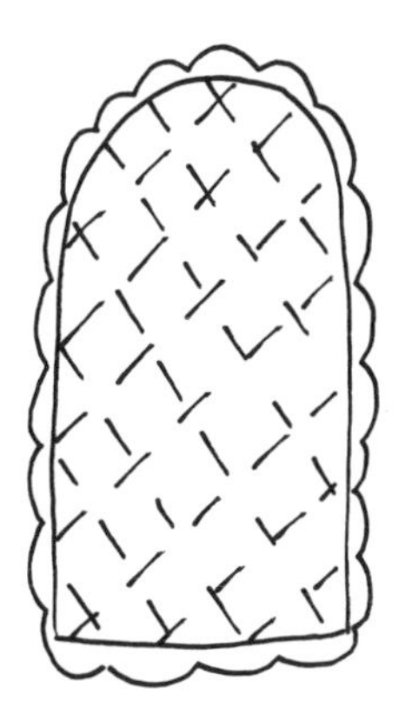

**4** Work your stitch design onto the front patterned piece of combined fabric and wadding with embroidery thread. Remove the tacking stitches. Place the pieces right sides together and insert a loop of ribbon in the top of the cosy. Taking a 1.5cm (½in) seam allowance, machine stitch around the outside edge, leaving the bottom unstitched.

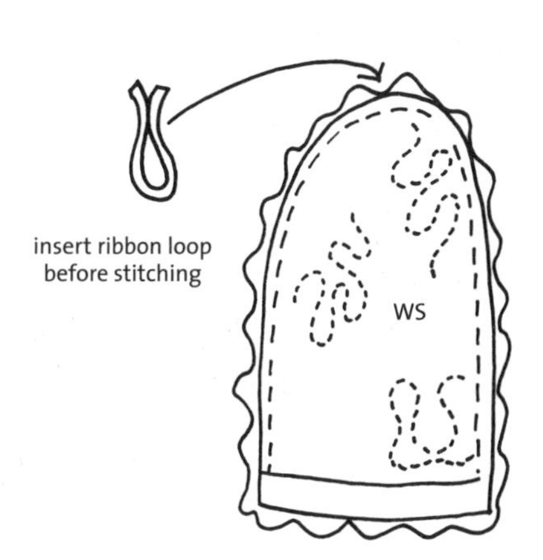

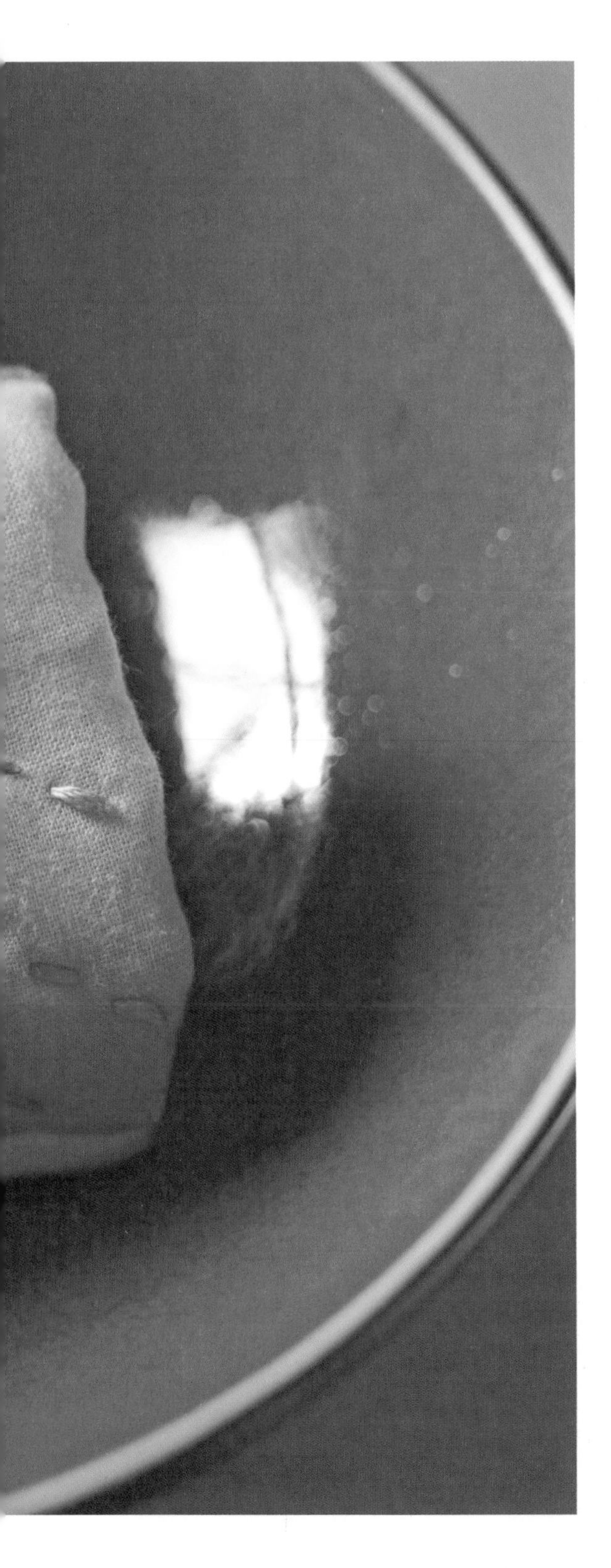

**5** Trim the bottom edge (the lining and the quilting) by 1.5cm (½in) and remove any excess fabric and wadding around the edges.

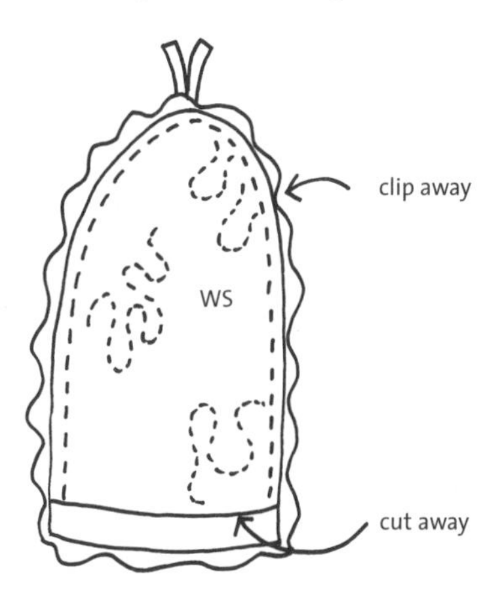


**6** Clip the curved top to allow ease. Fold under the outside layer of the base fabric twice to form a neat hem. Stitch this by hand all around.

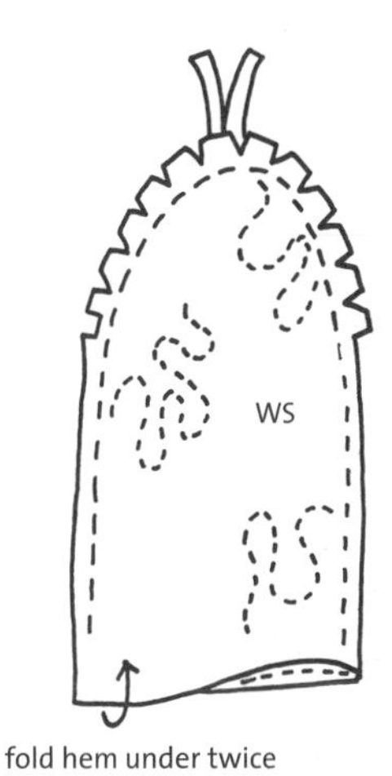


**7** Turn the cosy right sides out. If necessary, press lightly with a steam iron.

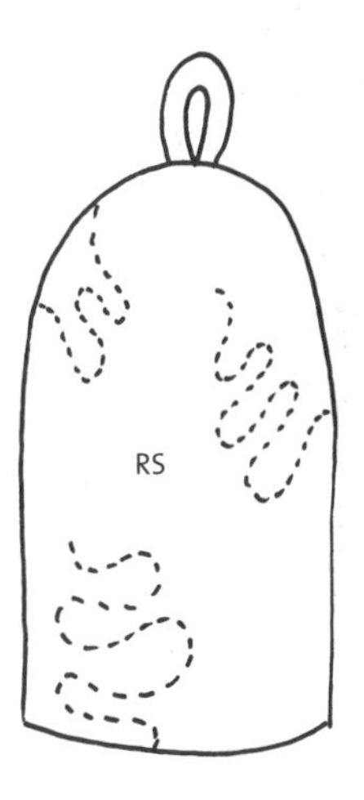

# cording

A great variety of designs can be created using cording techniques: the cords can be made individually and then bundled together for decoration or jewellery purposes; to add a creative twist, a number of cords can be plaited together to form a stronger cord that can be used as a handle or couched down onto a flat piece of fabric as decoration. A variety of different colours can be mixed together or, for a more sophisticated look, all of the cords can be the same colour. To embellish fabric they can be secured with hand or machine stitches or attached as ties or finishing touches on garments. Whichever way you use cords, they are sure to create a very distinctive decoration or textured fabric surface.

Thanks to modern technology you have choices about how you make cords. The easiest is to buy a cording and braiding foot for your sewing machine. This allows you to pass thin strips of fabric through a hole on the front of the foot. Using a zigzag stitch, the stitches wrap themselves around the fabric, pulling it tight. This creates a beautiful cord very simply. Another method is to cut your fabric into thin strips and, using a normal presser foot on the sewing machine, zigzag stitch over the fabric strip while you twist it into a spiral.

Different fabrics can be used to produce cords in a variety of thicknesses, textures and colours, so experiment and see what happens. I enjoy the effects of combining different colours and sometimes different fabrics in the cords that I make, and am quite happy to create bunches of cords for which I devise uses at a later date! They look good simply hanging from a peg in my workroom.

◀ Fine black and white Habutai silks form the twisted and opened cords here, stitched in rows to a silk base fabric.

# design samples

You can make cords to be used individually as a decorative feature, for example on bags or belts, or in bunches (for hat bands, curtain ties or jewellery, for example), or you can stitch, or couch, them by hand onto a piece of fabric to form an elaborate raised design or pattern.

Using different types of fabric produces markedly different effects so it is worthwhile experimenting to see what happens when you use, for example, a printed cotton fabric and a plain coloured fine felt fabric, cording the two different types of fabric together at the same time.

You don't have to use the cords in long lengths. Cut them up, knot them or wrap them around fabric strips, or try combining skinny cords with chunkier ones for a pronounced textural contrast. Use the cords in rows, looping them as you stitch, to make an attractive decoration for a textural cushion. Or stitch short lengths of cord in patterns on a pocket of a pair of jeans.

The process of cording and braiding can be a wonderfully inventive process. You can choose to plait the cords into different forms and thicknesses of braids, which could be used to trim garments or cushions.

A

▲ **Sample A:** This sample comprises cords made from combining narrow strips of printed cotton and coloured fine felt fabric in harmonious colours. The strips of fabric are simply folded and twisted as they are zigzag stitched on the machine (the stitching wraps itself around the fabric to form the cord).

B

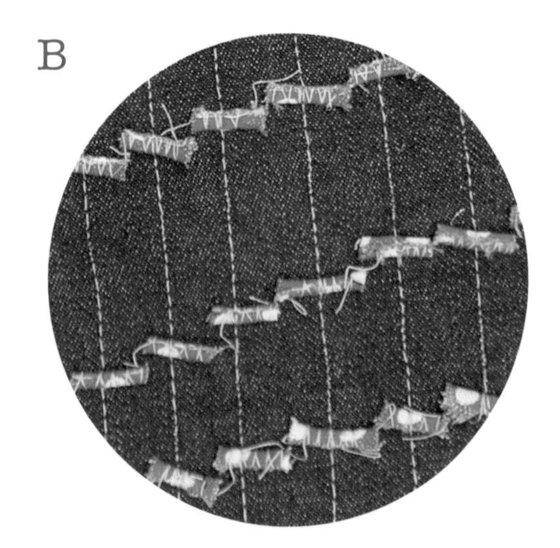

▲ **Sample B:** Here, fine cords are made in the same way as those in Sample A, but this time the cords are cut into short lengths and applied to a denim base fabric in regularly spaced stitched rows, the rows of contrast stitching holding the cords in place.

C

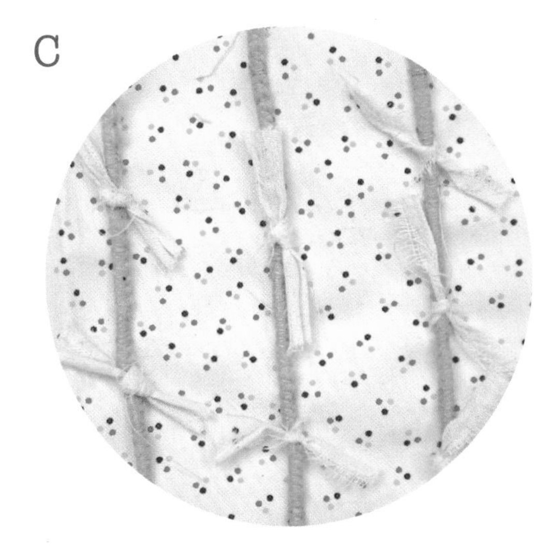

▲ **Sample C:** These cords are made from fine woollen fabric; they are stitched down in rows onto a printed cotton fabric using zigzag stitch. Strips of calico are threaded under the cord as it is stitched and then tied in a knot when the row is complete.

E

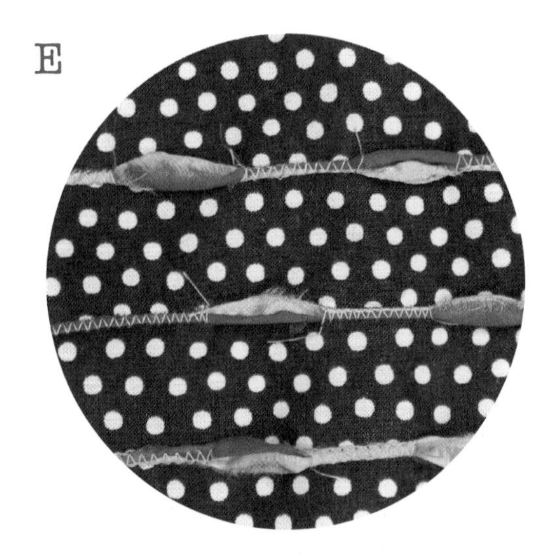

▲ **Sample E:** In this sample, torn strips of red chiffon and mustard-coloured silk are zigzag stitched directly onto a printed spot cotton. The stitching stops and starts at intervals so the fabric strips open to reveal the two colours.

D

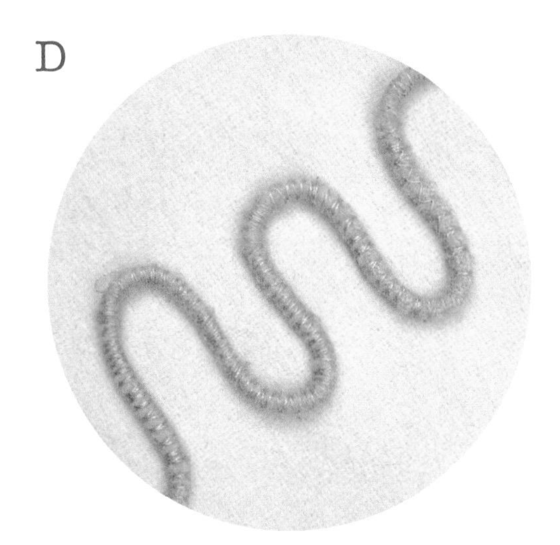

▲ **Sample D:** In this sample, thicker cord is made from a woollen felted fabric, zigzag stitched in the usual way, and machine stitched or hand couched to a woollen base fabric in a looped design.

F

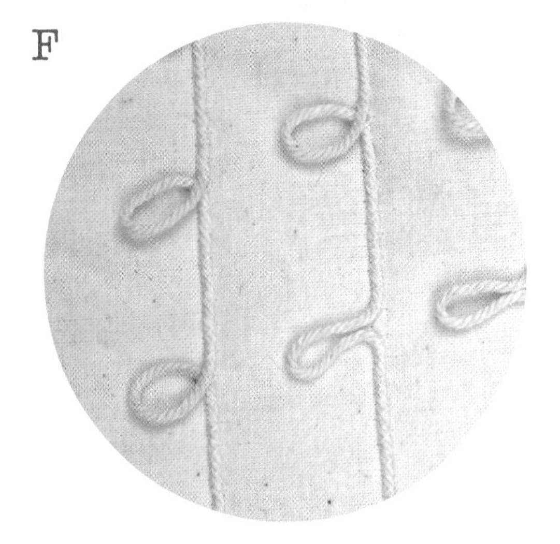

▲ **Sample F:** Here, ready-made fine cotton cord is zigzag stitched in rows onto a calico base. At intervals the machine is stopped, the presser foot raised and the cord pulled away to create a small loop before the line of stitching is continued.

# how to cord

You can make your own cords or you can purchase ready-made cord, such as piping cord, which is available in a variety of thicknesses. Making your own cord offers many more interesting design possibilities than working with ready-made cord.

**To make your own cords**

If you have a special cording and braiding foot, you can pass the fabric, cut into fine strips no more than 1.5cm (½in) wide, through the hole in the front of the foot (**1a**) and use a zigzag stitch to stitch over them. The zigzag stitch binds the fabric into a cord as you stitch. You can also make cords with a standard presser foot. Cut the strips in the same way. You will need to keep twisting the fabric strip as it passes beneath the presser foot so that the zigzag stitch binds the fabrics into a cord (**1b**). You can use one or two fabric strips to make each cord.

**Attaching cords to fabrics**

You will need to lay the cords down in your chosen positions and then secure them either by hand stitching or machine stitching. Couching is the technical term for this process.

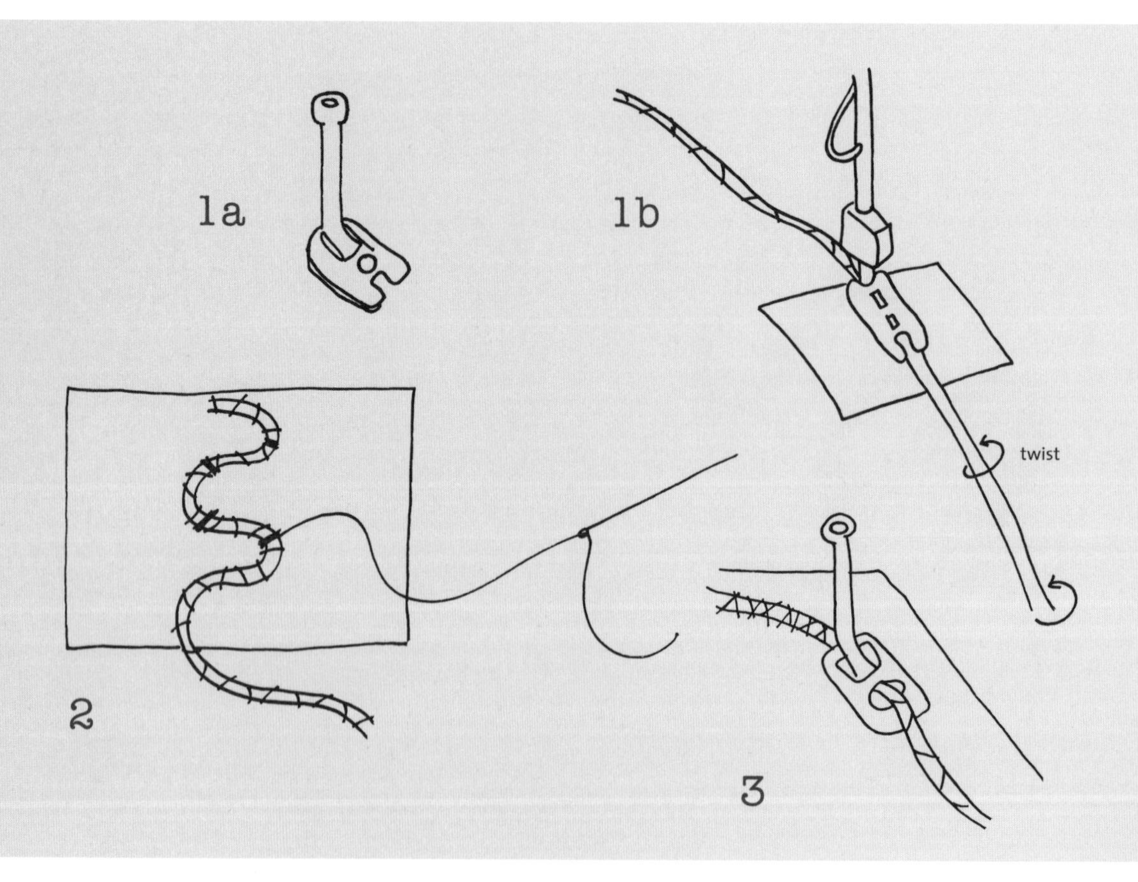

**Hand-stitching cords** Attach the cord to the fabric using small hand stitches (**2**). Why not try applying different types and thicknesses of cord to the fabric surface to create an exciting textural piece of work?

**Machine-stitching cords** Lay the cord down on the right side of the fabric and stitch over it using a zigzag stitch set to the widest setting (**3**).

**Variations**

When machine stitching the cord using the widest setting, it is possible to add further decoration by passing little strips of fabric underneath the stitched cord (**4a**), tying them to form a decorative knot on the surface (**4b**).

A decorative variation on machine-stitched couching is to stitch the fabric strip to the base fabric, then stop the machine at intervals, moving the fabric forward before resuming stitching (**5**). This creates a gap in the stitching and the fabric can unfurl naturally, as in Sample E on page 87.

You may prefer to use string or ready-made cord to apply to the surface of a fabric. In Sample F on page 87, ready-made cord has been attached as above, only this time when you stop stitching you leave the needle down in the fabric with the presser foot raised. You then pull the cord gently to create a loop before lowering the presser foot to stitch again (**6**).

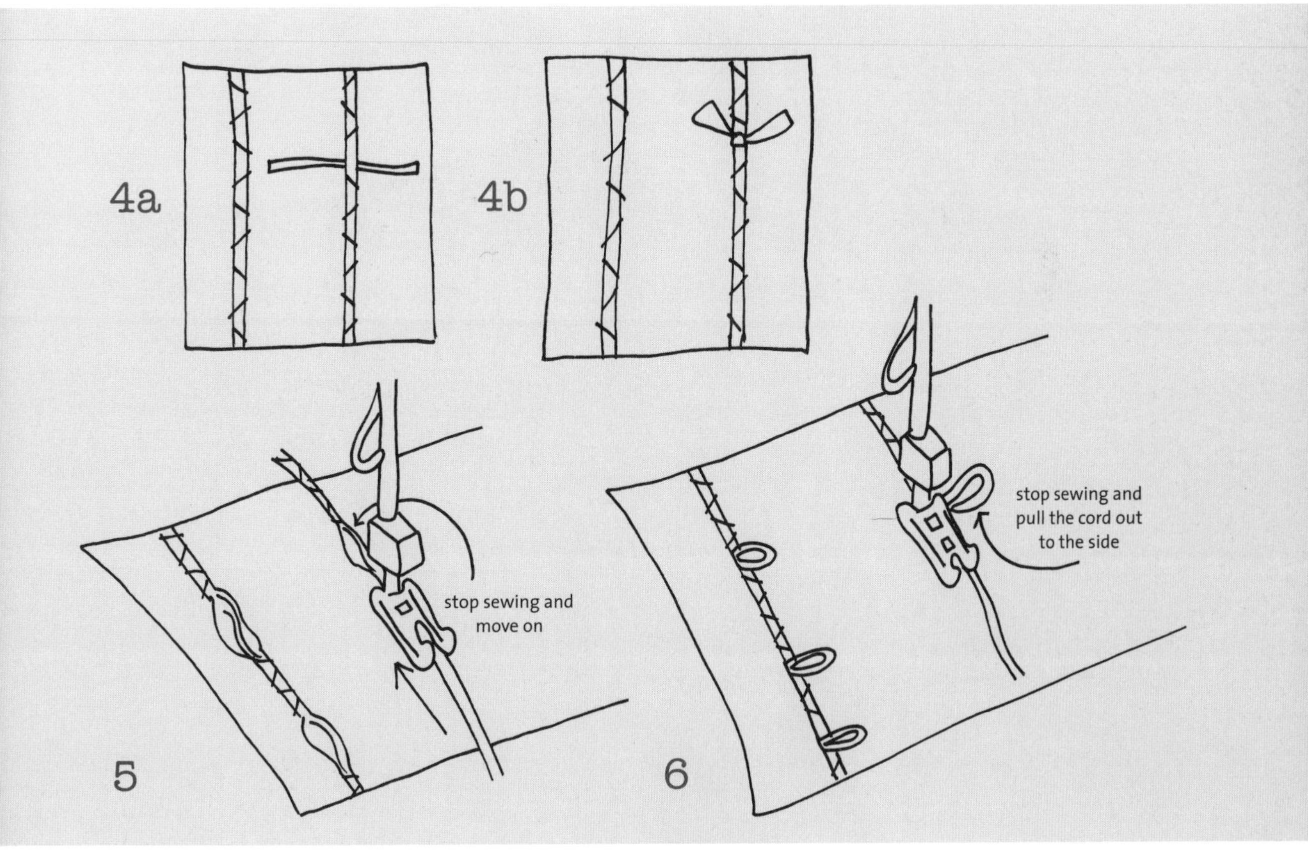

# corded hat braid

These cord bunches are very simple to make and look especially effective when two contrasting fabrics are used and the cords are twisted or plaited together to form a braid. Decide on the colours you are going to use as well as the different fabrics. You will then need to cut the fabrics into strips of, at most, 1.5cm (½in) wide and as long as required.

**What you need**

Two contrasting fabrics (a plain cotton and a printed cotton, for example), in contrasting colours; hat with a brim; tape measure; contrasting narrow ribbon to tie the cords together.

**Making the cord braid**

**1** Measure the circumference of the hat and decide how long you want to make the cord decoration. On this hat, I twisted the cords and allowed them to hang down several inches at the side.

**2** Make approximately 10 cords to roughly the same length, some from plain fabric and some from printed fabric.

**3** Twist the cords together, fold and machine stitch across the bundle of cords (to fit the hat).

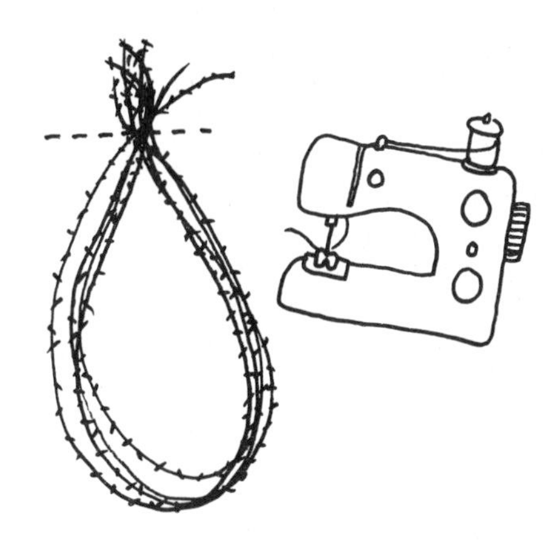

**4** Fit the stitched cords over the hat, trim as required, and tie a length of ribbon over the stitched join.

# plaited variation

You can plait three lengths of cord together to create a plaited braid. For a chunkier braid, plait three groups of five cords, as shown below.

# ● corded cushion cover

This corded cushion cover has been created using a plain cotton fabric and closely spaced rows of ready-made piping cord, machine-couched in place. The cushion back has a simple envelope closure. The cushion measures 40cm (16in) square.

**What you need**

Enough fabric to cover the cushion front and back, and to allow an overlap on the back; enough cord for the number of rows of cord used plus 50 per cent extra for the loops; fabric-marking pencil; ruler; matching thread; cushion pad, 40cm (16in) square.

**Cutting out the pieces**

**1** Cut out the fabric for the cushion cover front, 40cm (16in) square, plus 1.5cm (½in) seam allowances all around. Cut out two pieces for the envelope back flaps, each measuring 43 x 30cm (17 x 12in).

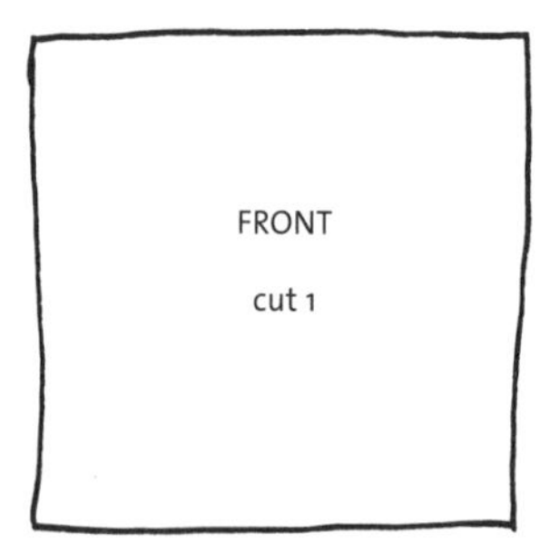


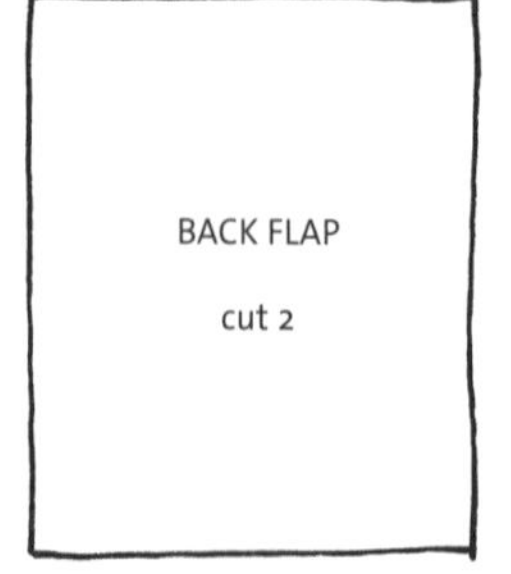


**Making the front cover**

**2** On the right side of the front fabric, using a fabric marking pencil and a ruler, mark out the positions along the top and bottom for the rows of cording.

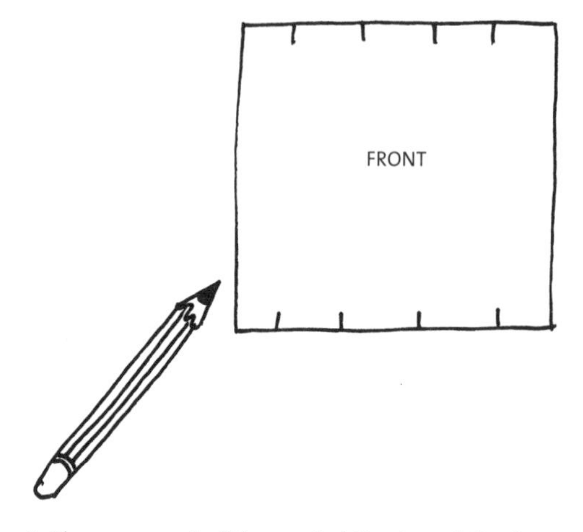


**3** Place one end of the cord at the top of the first marked position on your cushion front, right side facing up. Using zigzag stitch, begin to stitch the cord onto your fabric. Every 2.5cm (1in) or so, stop stitching, leaving the needle down in the fabric, and lift the presser foot up. Carefully pull the unstitched cord to form a little loop to sit on the surface of the fabric. Lower the presser foot again and continue sewing. Repeat for the entire length of the row and cut off the cord. Continue to work rows of looped cords over the surface of the cushion front.

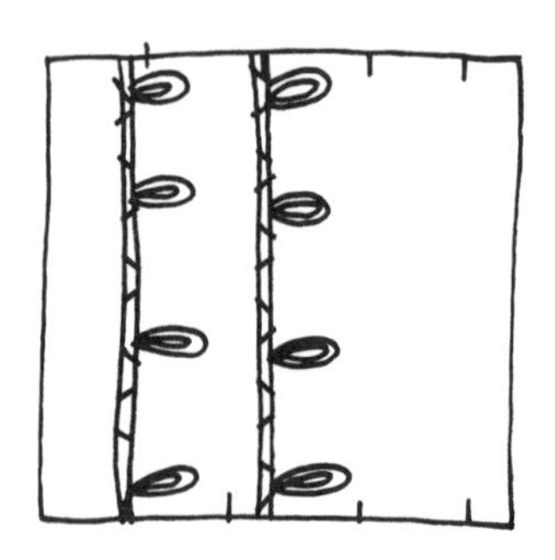

**Making the cushion back**

**4** On one of the long sides of each piece of back fabric, fold over a small hem twice onto the wrong side, pressing each fold in place with an iron. Topstitch the double folded hem in place using the sewing machine.

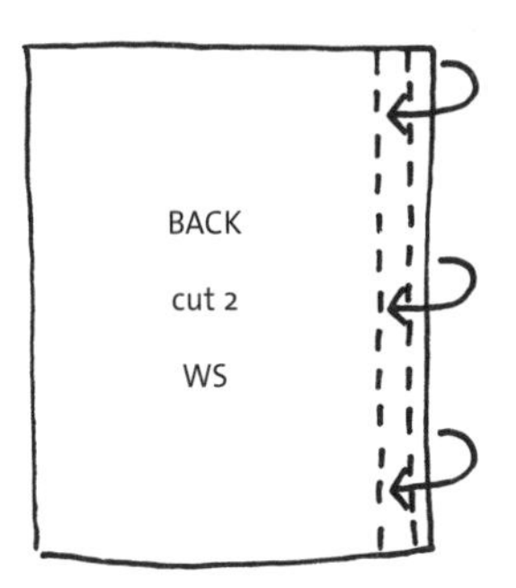


**5** Place one of the back flap pieces, right side facing down, on top of the cushion front. Match up the outer corners of the cushion front and the back flap so the hemmed edge is just past the centre of the cushion front.

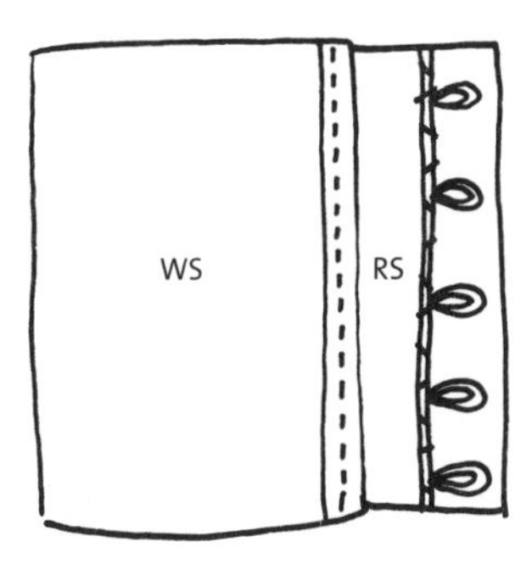


**6** Repeat this for the second back piece so that the two pieces overlap. Using a straight stitch, machine stitch the flaps and cushion front around the outer edges, leaving a 1.5cm (½in) seam allowance.

**7** Turn the cushion right side out and insert the cushion pad through the opening at the back.

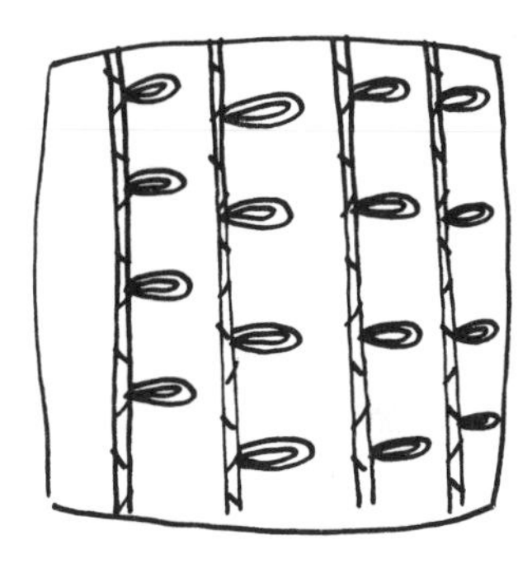

● ● ● **TIP**

If you wish, use a contrasting colour of thread to hem the back flaps of the cushion. Make little loops from the cord for buttonholes and stitch three or four buttonholes along the edge of the top flap at the back of the cushion. Stitch on matching buttons.

# kimono with corded tie

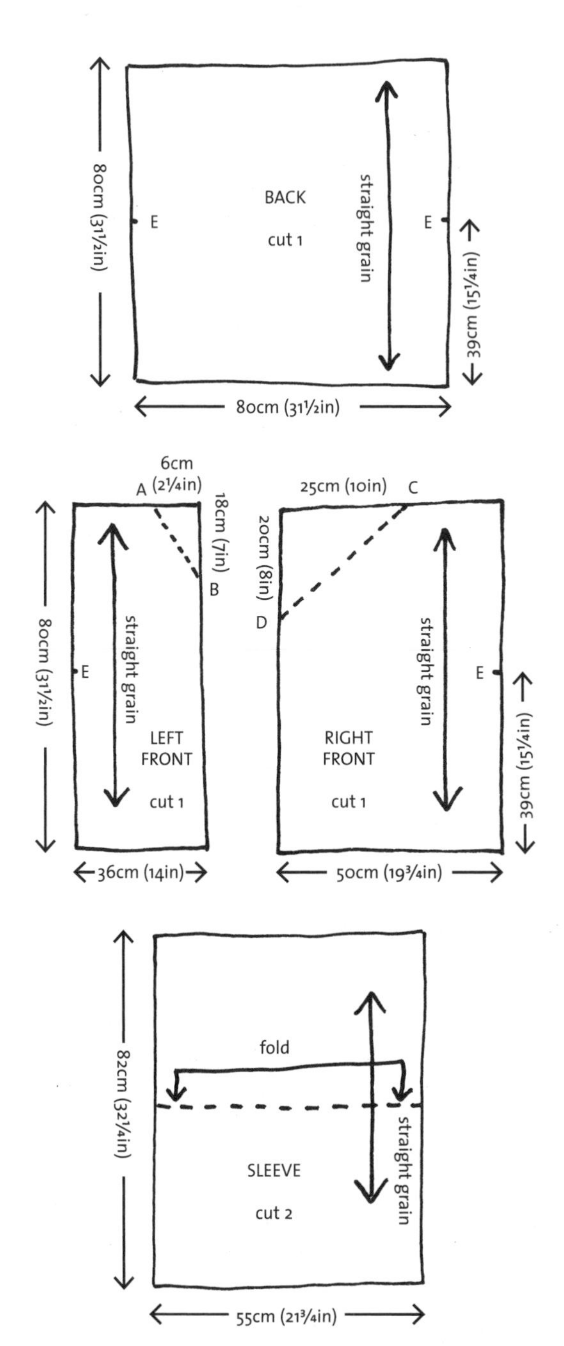


**Note** Add 1.5cm (½in) seam allowance to all measurements.

This kimono, lined in a contrasting fabric, has an exquisite corded tie. If you make the kimono in a thicker fabric, you could avoid lining it (making it easier to complete) but the contrasting lining does provide a wonderful finishing touch. The kimono shown here measures 76cm (30in) wide and 76cm (30in) long.

**What you need**

Patterned cotton fabric; plain cotton fabric for lining; two plain silk fabrics for cording. To make the kimono shown here, you will need approximately 3m (3¼yd) of each fabric for the kimono and tie belt, plus an additional 0.25m (¼yd) of two contrasting silks for the cording detail; tailor's chalk; matching thread.

**Cutting out and marking the pieces**

**1** In the main fabric, cut the back, left and right fronts and two sleeves to the measurements shown. Repeat for the lining. Lay the two front pieces out flat. Using tailor's chalk, mark the measurements for the neck (A–B, C–D) shown left and cut off the corners on the dotted line. Mark the armhole points (E) on the side seams.

**Making the sleeves**

**2** Separately fold over the long sides of each sleeve with right sides together. With a 1.5cm (½in) seam allowance, stitch together the longest sides of each sleeve (this forms the under part of the sleeves).

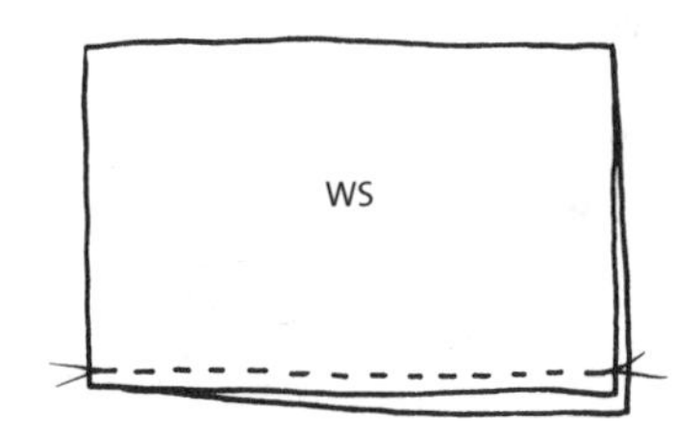

**Making up the kimono (top fabric)**

**3** Lay the back piece down, right side up. Place the two front pieces on top of the back, right sides down, as shown. With a 1.5cm (½in) seam allowance, stitch each side of the kimono from the bottom to the armhole point (E). Then match up the shoulder seams and stitch each front to the back.

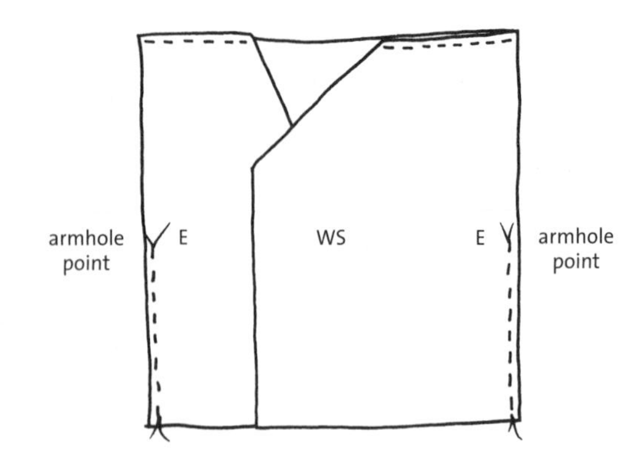


**4** With right sides facing, insert the first sleeve into the body of the kimono. Matching the seams, pin and then stitch, with a 1.5cm (½in) seam allowance all the way around. Repeat for the second sleeve.

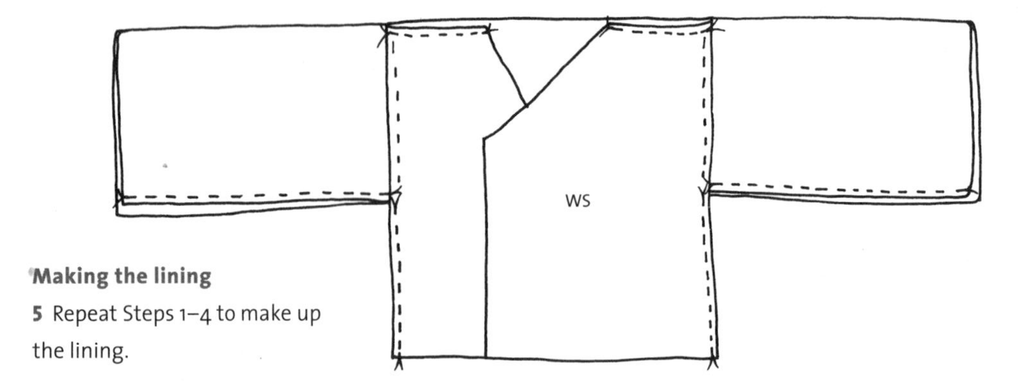


**Making the lining**

**5** Repeat Steps 1–4 to make up the lining.

**Lining the kimono**

**6** With the kimono and the lining placed together, right sides facing, first stitch the kimono and lining together along the hem, with a 1.5cm (½in) seam allowance. Then insert the lining inside the main body of the kimono, right sides facing (see below). Pin and then stitch together the kimono and lining fronts with a 1.5cm (½in) seam allowance. Press seams flat. Stitch the sleeve hems together, also with a 1.5cm (½in) seam allowance.

**7** Turn the kimono and lining right sides out and from this point treat as one garment. The neck area of the kimono is unstitched at this point.

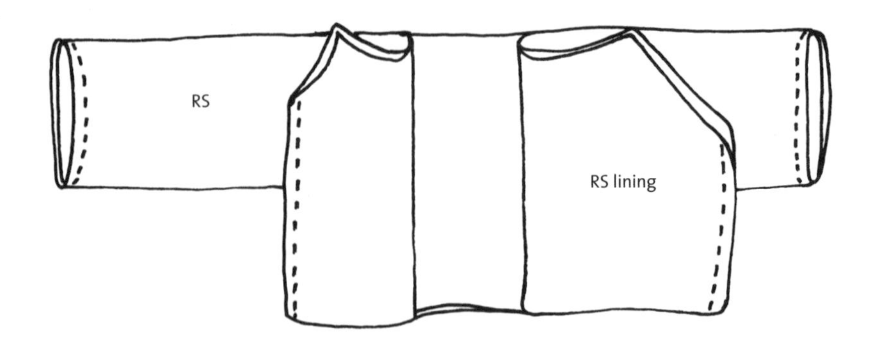

## Making the neckband

**8** Cut a piece of main fabric to measure 95 x 7cm (3ft x 2½in). Cut a matching piece of lining fabric. With right sides together, and with 1.5cm (½in) seam allowance, stitch top and lining fabrics together along one long side and two short sides. Clip the corners back and turn right side out. Press.

WS

## Joining neckband to kimono

**9** Fold under the raw edges of the neckband and, starting at the lower front of the narrower front panel, match up the corners and pin the neckband to the kimono, encasing the raw edges of the kimono in the open side of the neckband.

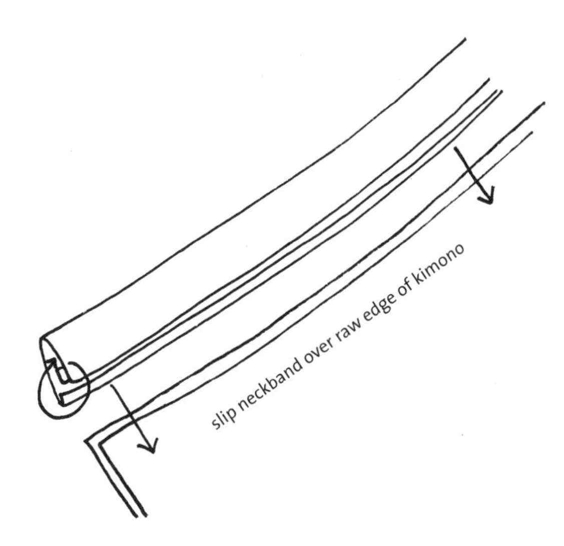


**10** Re-pin all of these layers together.

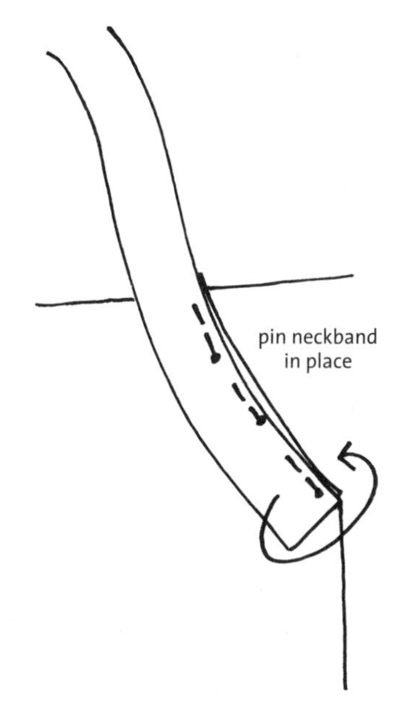


**11** Topstitch all of the way around. You will have a long flap on the left-hand side.

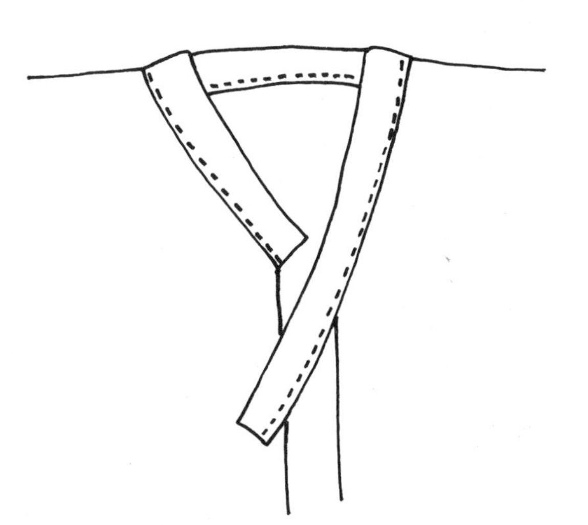

### Making the tie

**12** Cut a strip each of main fabric and lining, measuring 1m x 9.5cm (1yd x 3¾in), plus 1.5cm (½in) seam allowance all around.

**13** Attach and cord the two thin strips of silk (see page 89) to the right side of the patterned fabric in three evenly spaced rows.

**14** Place the corded top fabric strip right side down on top of the lining fabric, pin, then stitch together around all edges, taking a 1.5cm (½in) seam allowance and leaving a 10cm (4in) gap. Clip the corners and turn inside out.

**15** Press the belt flat and slip stitch the gap through which the belt was turned.

### ● ● ● TIP

To add a finishing touch, hand stitch a length of narrow Petersham ribbon in a matching colour around the inside of the neckband where it joins the kimono. This will cover any stitching as well as reinforce the neckline in a decorative way. You can hem the Petersham ribbon in place or secure it all around the edge with neat little running stitches in a contrasting thread.

# hand-stitch marks

● ● ● ● ● ● ● ● ● ● ● ●

My definition of hand stitching, actually a very simple type of embroidery, is a loose and creative type of mark-making using thread. The results have a unique personal quality that is very different from the marks made on a sewing machine. Whilst a sewing machine is quicker and the stitches produced are all of a regular length and width, hand stitch is unique, very much like your own handwriting.

Hand stitching combines particularly well with appliqué. Several of the design samples in this chapter are appliquéd, whereby small (sometimes tiny) cut and folded shapes or strips of fabric are applied to the base fabric with simple but effective hand stitches.

Stitching by hand is also a great way to create your own patterns on fabrics, using repeating rows of similar or different stitches. Variety can be introduced in the types and thicknesses of threads and yarns used, from sewing threads and embroidery silks to woollen yarns.

There are many forms of hand stitch but you can easily create new stitches of your own. In this chapter I have used a few simple hand stitches to produce interesting results with appropriate threads and fabrics. Of course, you can experiment with any stitches you like. Hand stitches can be worked on any fabric, from fine cotton lawns to heavy wools and tweeds, and even leather, provided you choose the right threads and suitable needles.

Although hand stitching is slow at first, with a little time and patience your skill quickly develops and the results become professional-looking.

◀ Small, irregularly shaped parcels of black felt have been scattered over white cotton voile. Each is secured with a few hand stitches in white sewing thread.

# design samples

This chapter looks at some simple hand-stitching techniques combined in many cases with appliqué. I have used hand-stitched patterns to form overall repeating designs. Some of the samples use the same type of hand stitch. However, by using different types of fabric, thread and pattern formations, it is possible to create strikingly different effects.

The range of projects that can be made from hand-stitched textiles is endless, from tiny decorations to surprisingly large items, such as quilts or throws.

If you have not done any hand stitching before, it is important to relax and not worry about making mistakes. Many people become tense when learning to stitch by hand and this can be carried into their work. You may find that certain types of stitches come more naturally to you than others. Experiment with different techniques and scales of stitch. Use thread singly or double it up to make a thicker thread. It really doesn't matter what you try, as you will always create something interesting. Hand sewing is very similar to drawing – you have simply substituted a needle and thread for your pencil.

Occasionally, you may find it helpful to keep the fabric taut while stitching – for example, while producing rows of similar stitches – as it makes it easier to produce regularly sized stitches. You can do this using an embroidery hoop (see page 132).

A

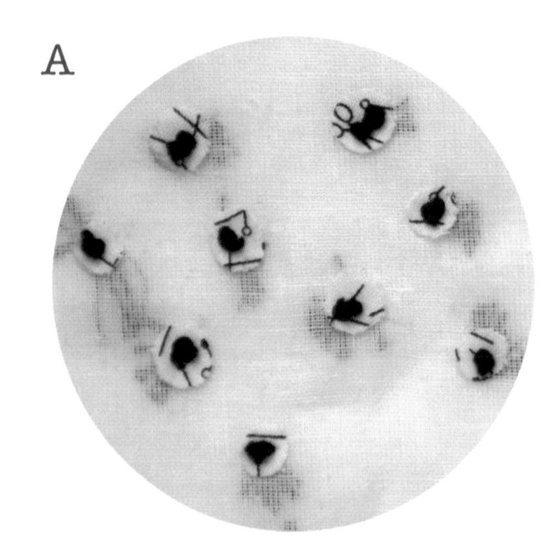

▲ **Sample A:** Here, tiny circles of cream and black printed cotton are randomly placed onto the calico base, and attached with a French knot in black sewing thread. The circles can be of any size and you can sew more than one French knot on a circle.

B

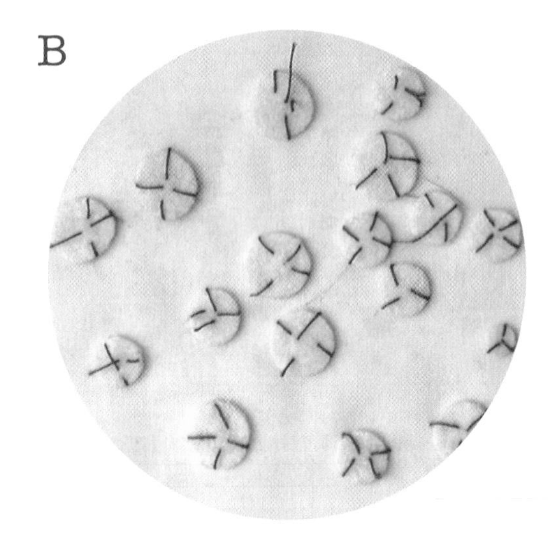

▲ **Sample B:** Here, two contrasting fabrics – a fine silk organza for the base and a thick wool for the circles – have been used. The circles were created with a revolving hole punch and were then randomly stitched in place on the base fabric using a few simple stab stitches in contrasting thread.

C

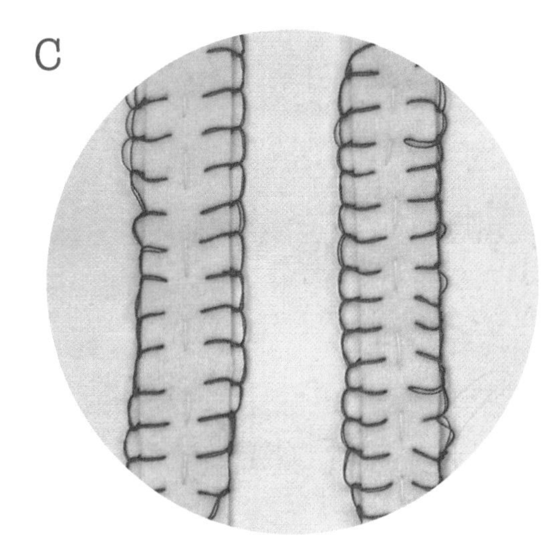

▲ **Sample C:** A lace-like effect has been created in this sample. Thin strips of silk have been blanket-stitched along their edges to the base cotton fabric. The sewing thread is used double. Instead of pulling the thread tight, the stitches are left loose, adding to the quirky, delicate effect.

E

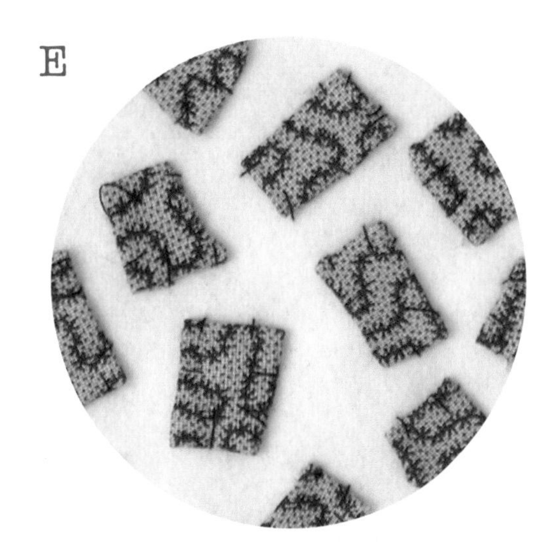

▲ **Sample E:** Here, little squares are made from folded parcels of printed cotton, randomly placed onto a woollen base with a few simple stitches in black sewing thread. To vary this, try changing the fabrics as well as the spacing between the squares.

D

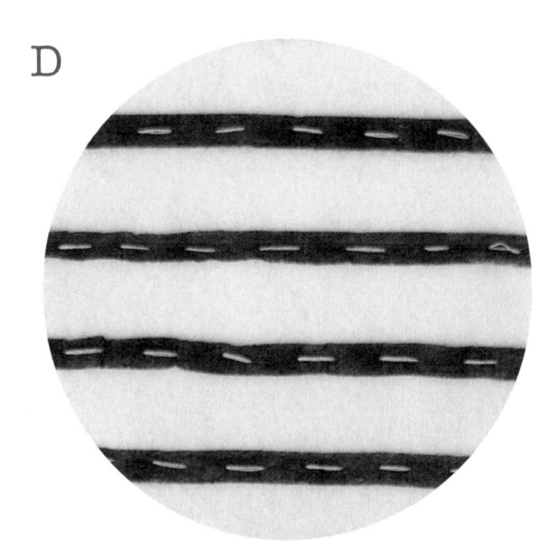

▲ **Sample D:** For this sample, black ribbon yarn is stitched in equally spaced rows on white wool, using running stitches in contrasting white thread. This simple technique would lend itself to many different variations of colour and stitch.

F

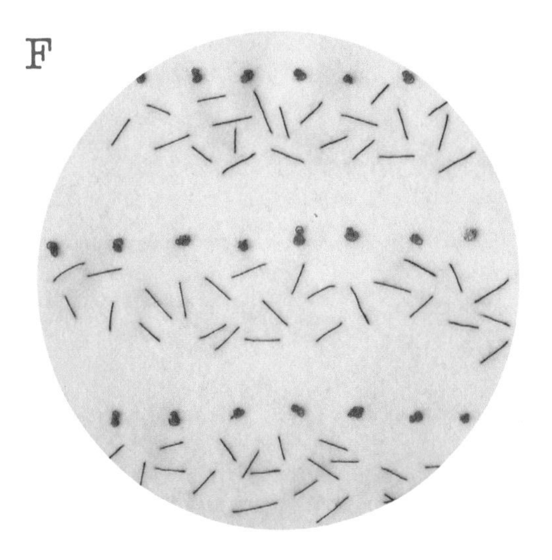

▲ **Sample F:** Here, two stitch styles are used to create an interesting textural effect on a white woollen base. French knots are worked in a double strand of red sewing thread in regularly spaced rows; stab stitches are worked in a single strand of black sewing thread.

# how to hand stitch

Your choice of fabric will dictate the size of the hand-sewing needle you need to use. The general rule is to use a fine sharp needle for hand sewing delicate, lightweight fabrics and to use a thicker sharp needle for heavier weights of cloth. If you find it difficult to pass the needle through the fabric, use a thimble.

**Basic stitches**

I like to match simple stitches with good quality fabric to produce exciting results.

**Running stitch** This simple stitch is quick to work. With a knot in the end of the thread, bring the needle and thread through from the back to the front of the fabric (**1a**). Now simply run the needle and thread in a straight line along the fabric, pulling the needle through after each group of stitches. You may choose to sew stitches of the same (**1b**) or different lengths.

**Blanket stitch** This stitch can be used as a decorative feature or as a securing stitch to prevent fabric fraying and to neaten raw edges. Decide

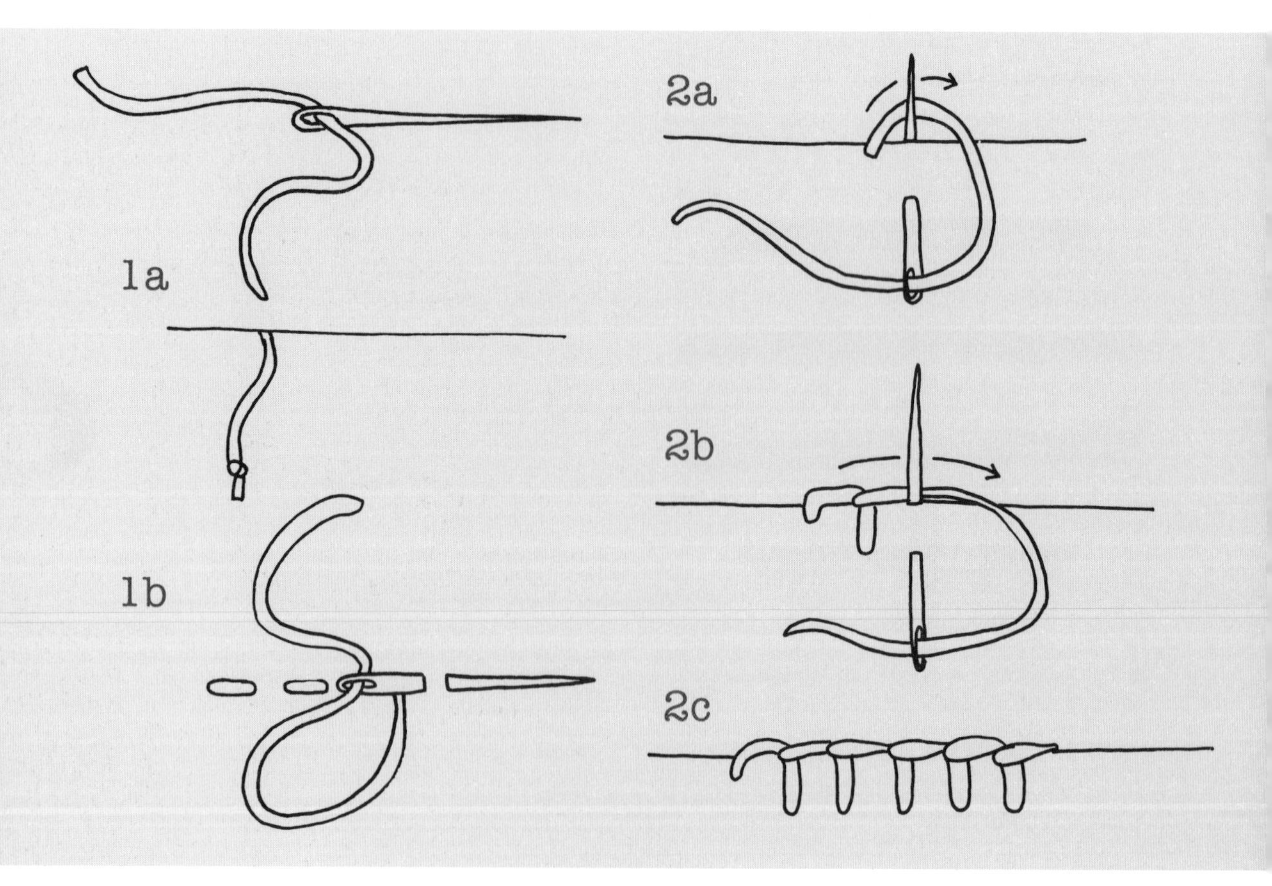

how long you want your stitches and how far you want to space them apart. Closely spaced stitches resemble satin stitch, whereas a lacier effect is achieved by wider spacing.

Take the needle from the back to the front of the fabric close to the fabric edge. Then take the needle to the back of the fabric, passing the thread under the needle and pulling the needle through (**2a**). Repeat this process making sure that the thread passes under the needle each time (**2b**). Repeat until you have the required number of stitches (**2c**).

**Stab stitch** This stitch is simple but very effective. Follow the method as for running stitch (**1a**), only this time place the stitches randomly on the surface of the fabric (**3**). You may choose to sew directly on the fabric or you may use stab stitch to attach cut shapes to a base fabric (**4**), as in Samples B, E and F on pages 104 and 105.

**French knots** These are little bobbles of thread on the surface of a piece of fabric. Their size depends on the thickness of thread used: the finer the thread, the smaller the knot will be.

Bring your needle and thread to the front of the fabric. Take a small stitch and, holding the thread taut, wrap the thread around the needle 2–3 times (**5a**). Swivel the needle to go back through the same hole, keeping your finger on the wrapped threads as you do so. Use your finger to push the wrapped thread down off the needle (**5b**). Take the needle to the back of the fabric through the knot (**5c**), leaving the stitch sitting on the fabric surface (**5d**).

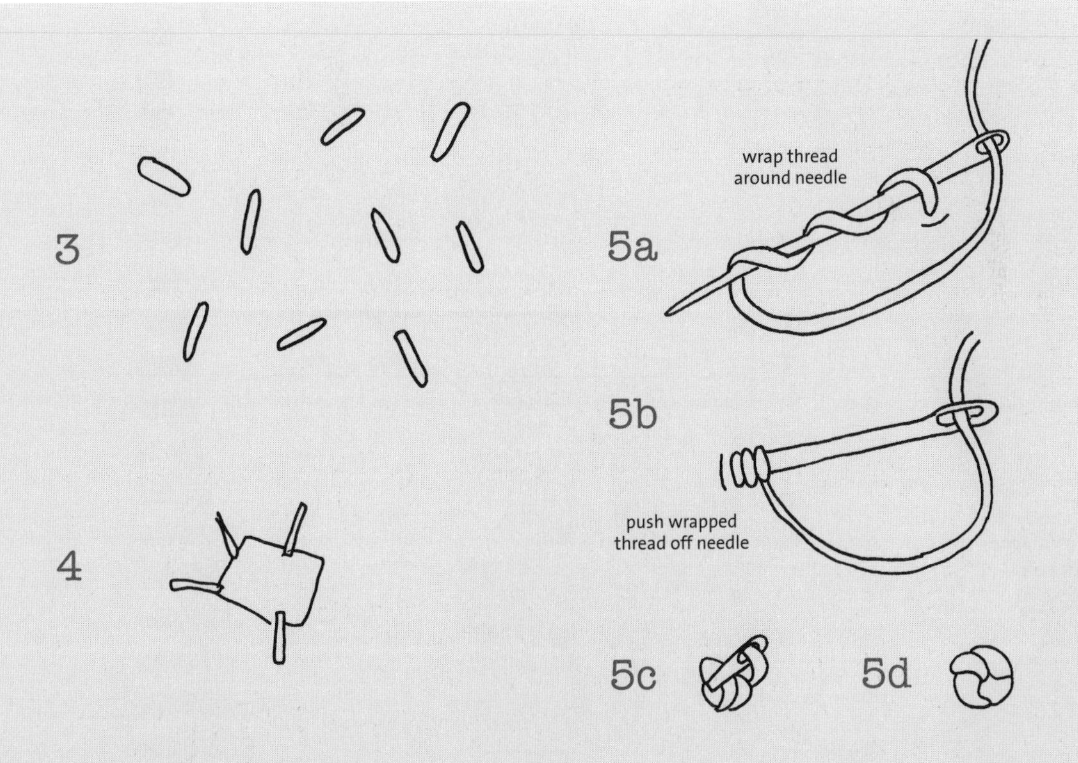

# drawstring bag

This versatile bag can be used to hang cherished possessions on a wardrobe door handle or to store the clothes pegs in the laundry. Change the colours to suit the setting or make several to hang on a coat rack in the hallway. The little circles are attached to the top fabric using French knots. Work out a rough design before cutting them out. The bag shown here measures 33 x 25cm (13 x 10in).

**What you need**

Plain cotton fabric for the bag; cotton fabric for the lining (matching or contrasting colour); patterned fabric for appliqué circles; revolving hole punch; ruler; fabric-marking pencil; six-stranded thread; sewing needle and thread; cord to hang the bag.

**Making the bag**

**1** Cut out two pieces of main fabric measuring 38 x 25cm (16 x 11in). Cut two pieces of lining fabric to the same size.

**2** Cut out little circles, from the patterned fabric, to the size and number needed for your design, using a revolving hole punch. Attach each circle onto the right side of the front part of the bag fabric in a random pattern, securing each with a French knot (see page 107) using matching six-stranded thread.

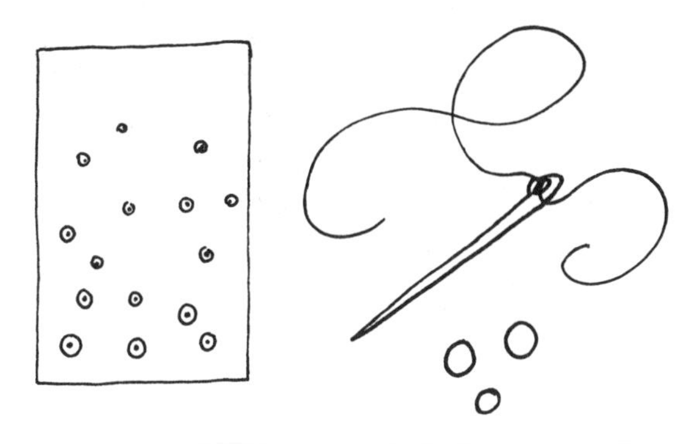

**3** Stitch the two pieces of main fabric together around the two sides and the bottom, taking a 1.5cm (½in) seam allowance. Leave the top open. Repeat for the lining fabric.

**4** Press open the seams and fold over 4cm (1½in) at the top of each to the wrong side and press.

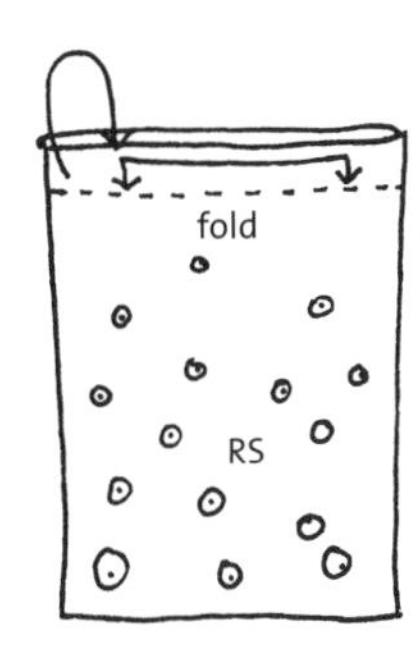


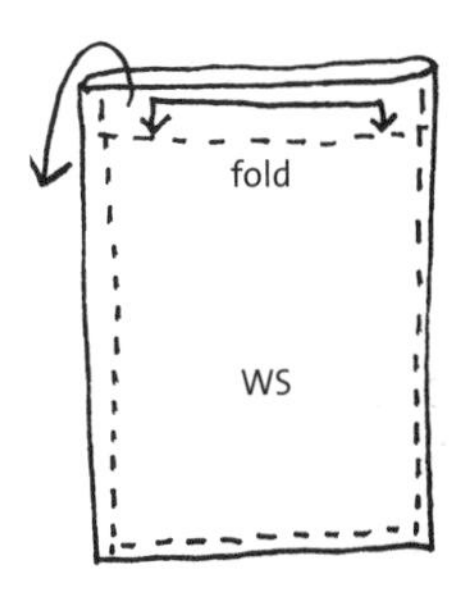

**5** Place the lining inside the outer bag and position it so that the top edge is revealed a little.

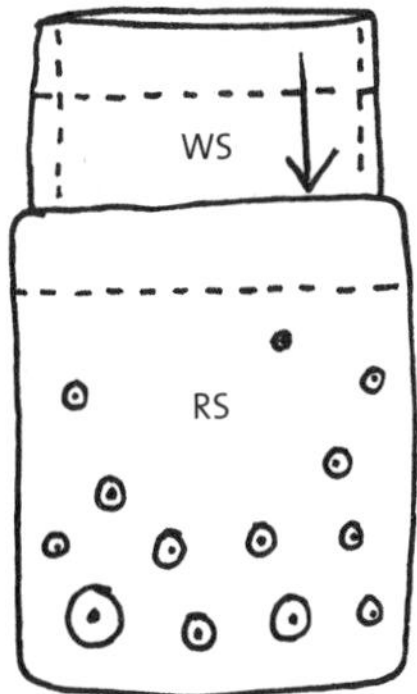


## Finishing the bag

**6** Separate the folds on the outer bag and lining and open out the fold on the outer bag. Punch two holes at equal distance on either side of the outer seam, approximately 2.5cm (1in) below the top edge. Using contrasting thread, work closely spaced blanket stitch around the raw edges (see page 106).

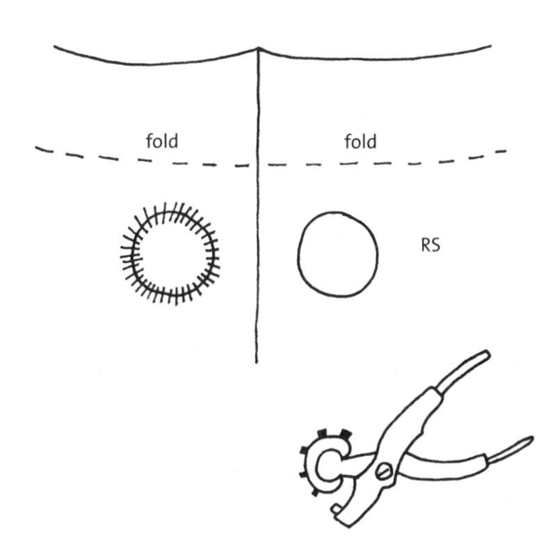


**7** Re-fold the top edges of the outer bag and lining along the point where they were pressed. Sew a straight stitch around the top of the bag and a second line of stitching about 2.5cm (1in) below to create a channel for the cord.

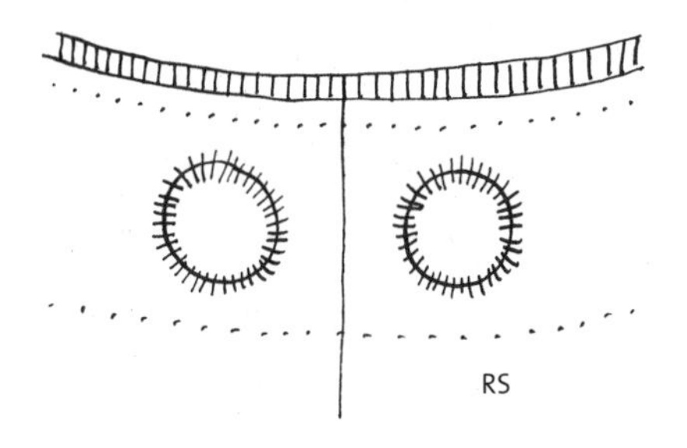


**8** Pass the cord carefully through the stitched holes and around the top channel of your bag. Make some little decorative ends for your cord. I used an enlarged version of the circles and French knots that decorate the bag.

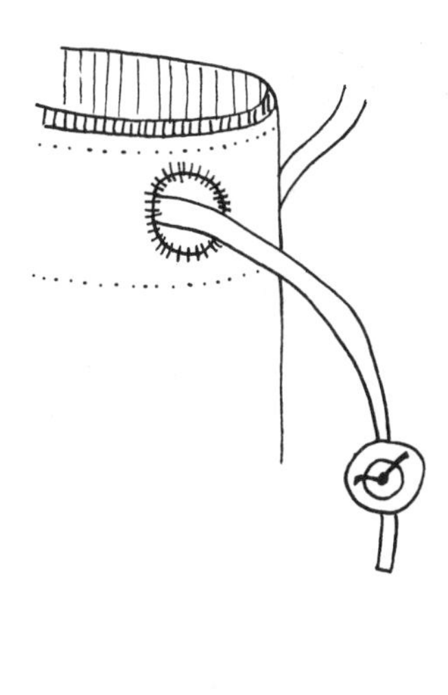

# lampshade trim

Before you start, decide on the width and placement of the strips in relation to your lampshade and on the size of the little parcels that will decorate the strips. Also, think about the colour of the fabric and thread you choose, as when the light shines through the shade it gives a wholly different look. This lampshade is 15cm (6in) deep, the strips are 6cm (2½in) wide and the parcels are about 2cm (¾in) square.

**What you need**
Small amounts of two types of fabric, one light fabric for the strips and one heavier fabric for the shapes (here black voile is used for the strips and black cotton for the squares); needle and matching sewing thread; fabric-marking pencil; fabric glue (optional).

**Preparing the fabric shapes**
**1** Cut the heavier fabric into pieces, approximately 2.5cm (1in) square. Fold the four sides inwards to the reverse side of the fabric, making a smaller square parcel with neatened edges.

**2** Carefully secure the folded edges in place on the reverse side of the fabric with a few stitches in matching thread. Avoid stitching through to the right side.

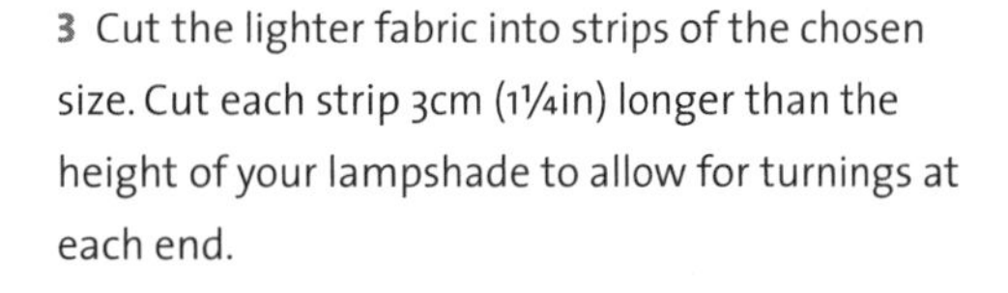

**3** Cut the lighter fabric into strips of the chosen size. Cut each strip 3cm (1¼in) longer than the height of your lampshade to allow for turnings at each end.

**4** Randomly place your prepared squares onto the strips and secure them in place, right side up, with stab stitches (see page 107).

**5** Mark the placement of the strips on the shade with a fabric-marking pencil. Then tuck the top edge of one strip over the top of the lampshade and secure with a few hand stitches or a dab of fabric glue. Repeat at the base of the shade, after gently pulling the strip so that it is taut, not slack. Repeat with the remaining strips.

# smocking

Smocking is a technique in which embroidery stitches are used to gather in fullness, usually across the yoke, cuffs or neckline of a garment, resulting in a natural elasticity. The technique is closely associated with the smocks originally worn by farm labourers, in which the yoke was gathered in with smocking stitches. Often the symbols of the owner's craft or trade were embroidered within the smocking on the yoke – a woodcutter's smock, for example, might depict leaves or trees.

Smocking has much the same effect as rows of gathering, but creates clearly defined pleats or folds in the fabric, so care needs to be taken when organizing the smocking stitch pattern. Generally, the amount of fabric gathered by the smocking is around three times the width of the finished article. When starting a project, work a test piece first to determine exactly how much the fabric will gather.

Lightweight fabrics with a stable weave, such as cottons, silks and fine woollens, are good choices for smocking as they gather well. Historically, smocking was also worked in piqué, crèpe de Chîne and cashmere. Although traditionally worked on plain fabrics, you can create some interesting effects with patterned fabrics, too.

Most smocking for home projects is done by hand using embroidery needles and threads (although you can find pleating machines that do a similar job). You can make your own stitch guides for the smocking or you can purchase iron-on transfers in haberdashery departments.

◀ Black sewing thread has been used to smock the folds of this plain cream fabric, creating a 3-D diamond effect.

# ● design samples

These samples demonstrate the sculptural effects that can be achieved by smocking different fabrics, from lightweight cottons and silks to heavier Melton wools. Some fabrics are easier to work with than others but generally smocking can be achieved using any fabric. A side benefit of smocking is that it transforms a flat, ungiving fabric into an elastic one, allowing ease without the necessity of determining a close fit.

When choosing a fabric for smocking, first consider how the fabric drapes. Stiff fabrics, like silk taffeta and cotton organdie, yield crisp, structured results. Lighter fabrics, such as cotton and lightweight wools, create the opposite effect, with more organic-looking results.

You also need to decide whether to use a matching or contrasting thread colour. Remember there will be two parallel lines of stitching for each fold or pleat, so choose your colours carefully. Do you want them to blend with your fabric or do you want them to make a specific colour statement?

The design samples here are just a few of the ways in which you can employ smocking. You could use it successfully for projects like aprons (to gather in the bib for example), on the top of a pocket or as a design feature on a curtain tie-back or a cushion.

There are many different decorative smocking stitches, the majority of the samples shown here use the basic honeycomb stitch, but other patterns are possible and the principle remains the same in each case.

A

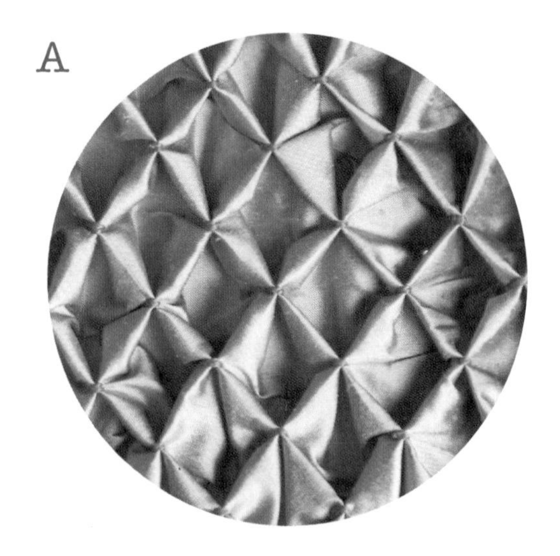

▲ **Sample A:** Here, silk dupion creates sharply defined smocked folds and an interesting play of light. It has been smocked with a contrasting scarlet sewing thread that highlights the honeycomb effect.

B

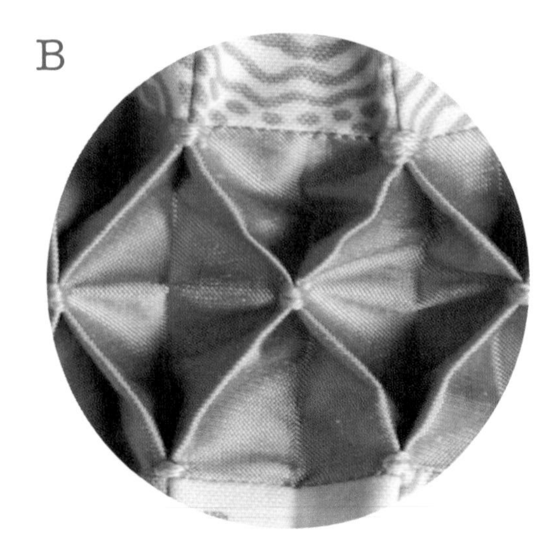

▲ **Sample B:** Silk dupion has been smocked here using a toning thread and the smocking has been patched with a lightweight printed cotton.

C

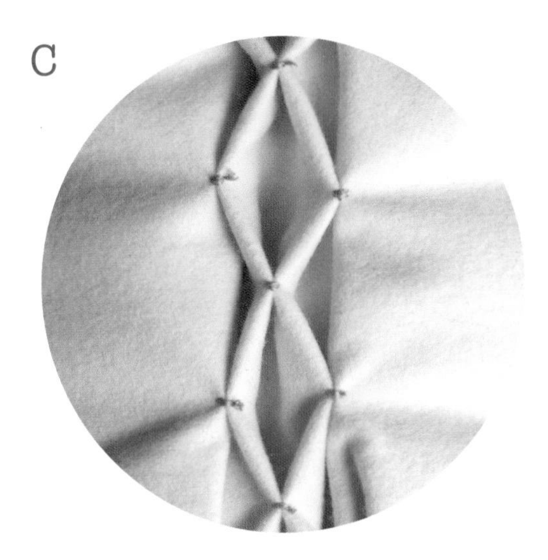

▲ **Sample C:** In contrast to the sharp folds in Samples A and B, here softer folds are created on a cream wool fabric. The smocking was created by using a contrasting coloured six-stranded embroidery thread.

E

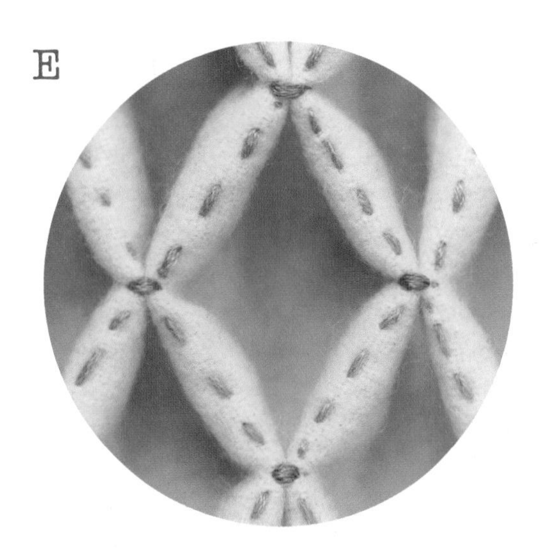

▲ **Sample E:** The same cream wool fabric as Sample C has been smocked with a contrasting six-stranded embroidery thread and given extra emphasis with running stitches in a second colour on top of each fold.

D

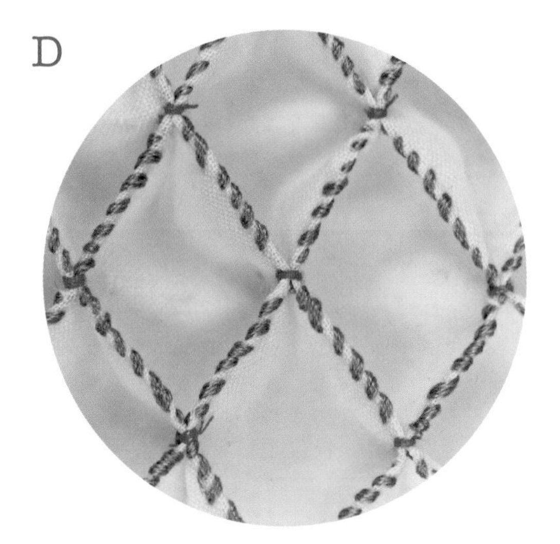

▲ **Sample D:** In this sample, the smocked diamond shapes are emphasized with over-stitching using a six-stranded embroidery thread in a contrasting shade.

F

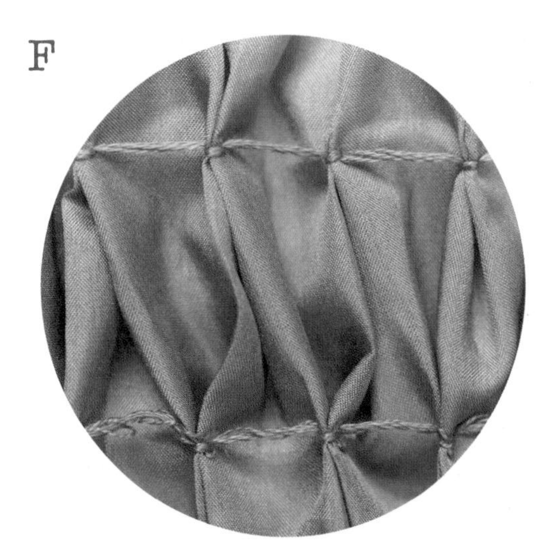

▲ **Sample F:** Here, a lightweight silk has been gathered into unstructured smocked folds, which are stitched in place with contrasting six-stranded embroidery thread: small smocking stitches are worked over the folds in the usual way, but the stitches joining them form rows across the front of the fabric.

# how to smock

As smocking is worked over folds in the fabric, you need to work out the size of these first. The size and number of folds will determine the quantity of fabric required (see Pleating, page 44).

### Preparing the smocking grid

Mark a piece of paper with a series of dots to represent the size of the chosen folds. Each fold requires two dots (to represent the front and back of the fold). Remember that the larger the space between the dots, the larger the smocking. Each dot represents a fold line. The dots are typically spaced evenly both horizontally and vertically. When the grid is complete, transfer the marks to your fabric. If your paper is not big enough for the smocked area, make photocopies and join together.

### Preparing the fabric for smocking

Place your fabric on a flat surface, right side down. Carefully pin the marked paper face up on the wrong side of the fabric.

To transfer the dots and mark the fabric, pierce the paper with a sharp pencil (**1a**). When you have marked the entire grid, thread a needle and knot

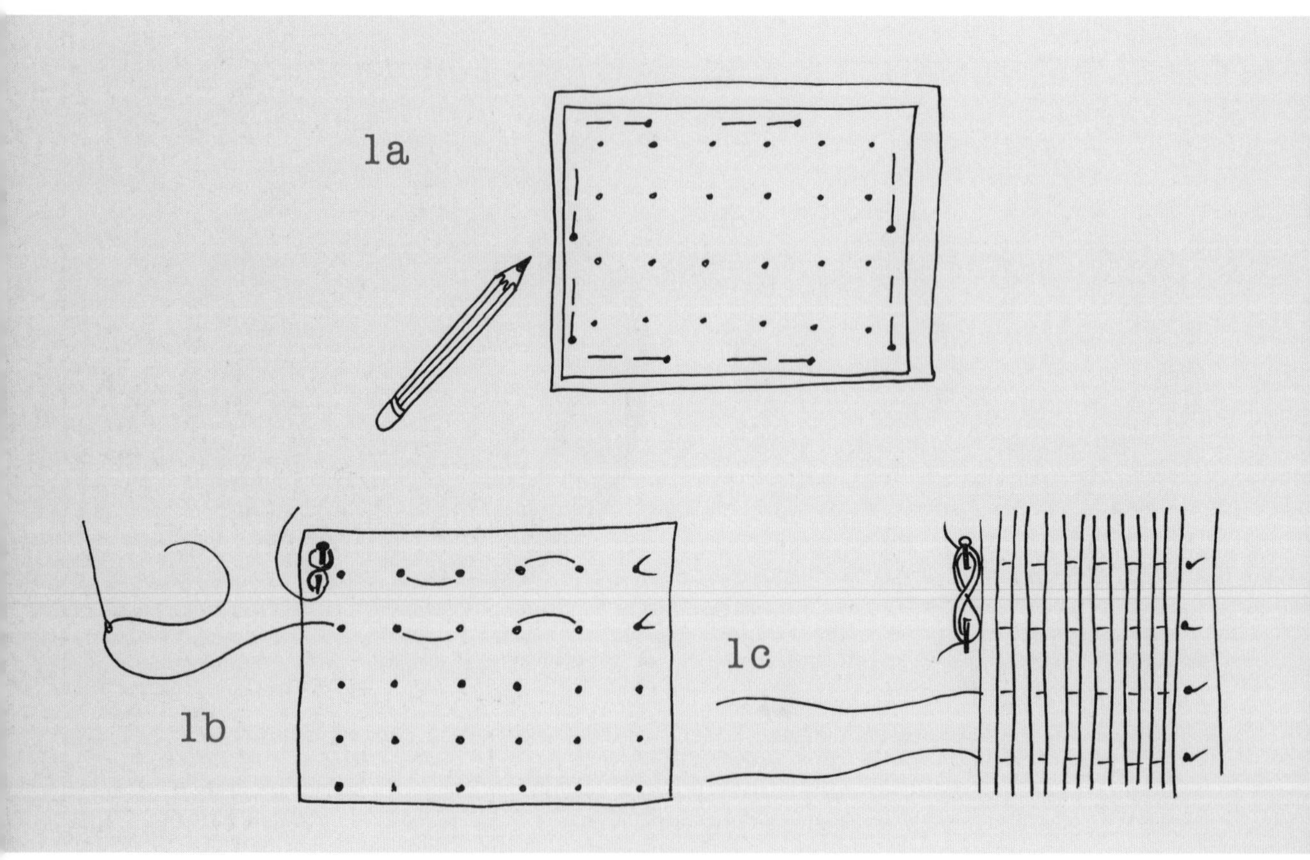

the end. Gather the fabric by joining the dots with running stitches (**1b**), taking the needle down at the first dot and coming up at the next dot. Continue until all the dots have been stitched. The stitches are removed when the smocking is complete.

Draw the threads to pull the fabric into even folds. To secure the folds, tie the loose thread ends and wrap them two at a time in a figure of eight formation around a dressmaking pin at one edge (**1c**). Turn the fabric over so that the right side is facing you. The fabric is now ready to smock.

### Smocking the fabric

There are various smocking stitches, but honeycomb stitch produces the most sculptural effect and is easy to work. It creates a series of diamond-shaped hollows across two pleats, caught at each corner of the diamond with a couple of stitches. Work from left to right, across two folds and up and down across two lines of gathering stitches. Bring the needle to the front of the fabric and backstitch over the first two folds (**2a**) a couple of times. Then work the smocking sequence (**2b**) by taking the needle down behind the folds to the second row of gathering stitches and stitch second and third folds together before bringing the needle back up again to the first row of gathering stitches, and repeating the process across all the folds. Repeat this on rows three and four of the gathering stitches (**2c**) until all the smocking is completed.

As an alternative to structured smocking, you could prepare the fabric for smocking in the usual way, but take the sewing thread across the folds in front rather than behind them (**3**).

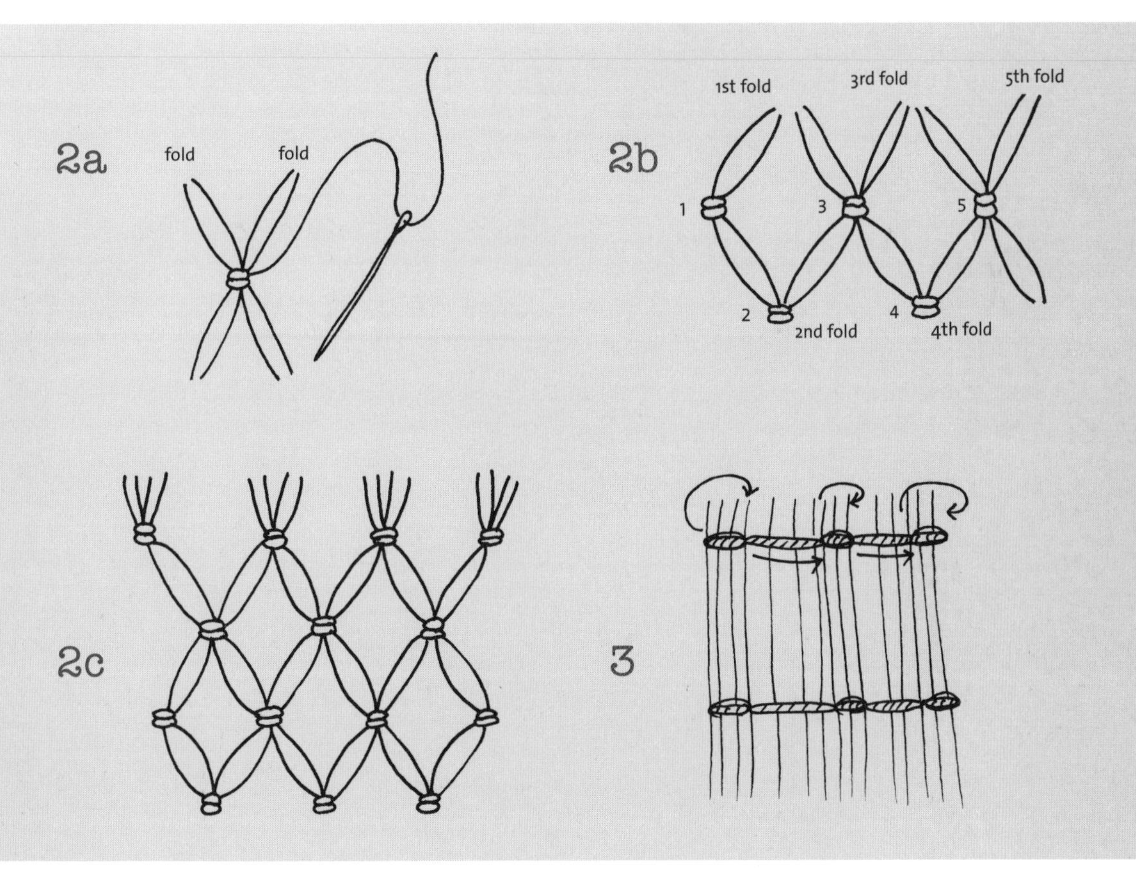

# cushion

This small cushion is made in a soft Melton wool, with just a few graphic smocking stitches pulling the centre into loose folds. It is smocked in a contrasting six-stranded embroidery thread. The cushion measures 36 x 28cm (14 x 11in) after smocking. Before smocking it measures 36cm (14in) square. Allow for 1.5cm (½in) seam allowances when calculating the fabric required.

**What you need**

Piece of cream woollen fabric for cushion front; heavyweight cream cotton fabric for backing; fabric-marking pencil; six-stranded embroidery thread in a contrasting colour; 36 x 28cm (14 x 11in) piece of wadding for stuffing.

**Making the cushion front**

**1** Cut out the cushion front measuring 36cm (14in) square, plus 1.5cm (½in) seam allowance all around. Make a paper template of the smocking grid (8 dots horizontally x 7 dots vertically), measuring 2.5cm (1in) between the dots.

**2** Mark the centre point of the fabric and align the centre of the grid on the wrong side of the fabric. Pin in place and mark the grid on the fabric (see page 118).

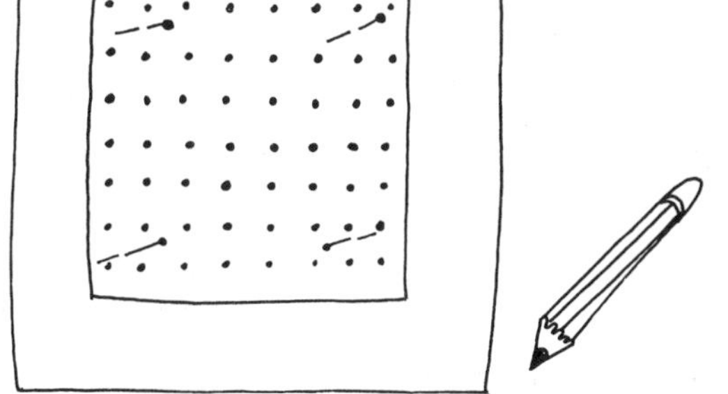


**3** Run a straight stitch through the row of dots on the wrong side of the fabric. Carefully gather the stitches to form the folds (see page 118).

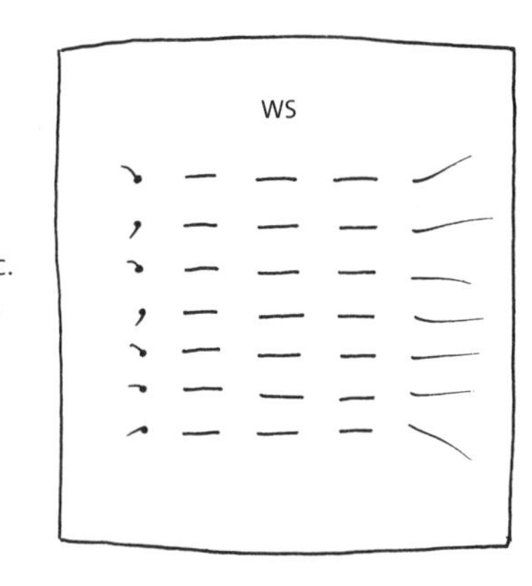


**4** Turn the fabric to the right side. Using six-stranded embroidery thread, start to work the smocking in a honeycomb pattern (see page 119) over the pleats, following the gathering stitch lines.

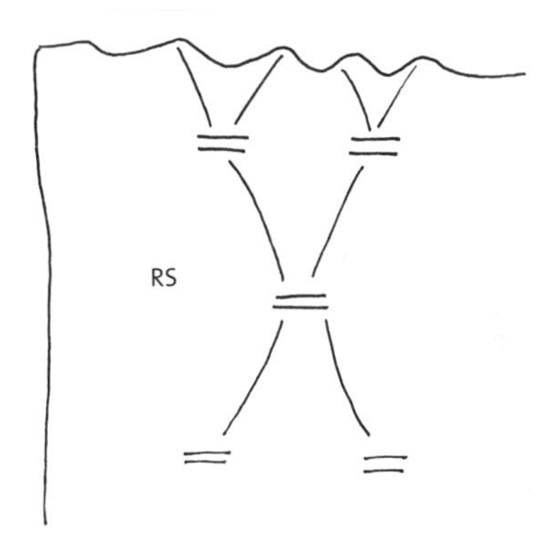


**5** Complete all seven rows of smocking stitches to finish the smocked pattern.

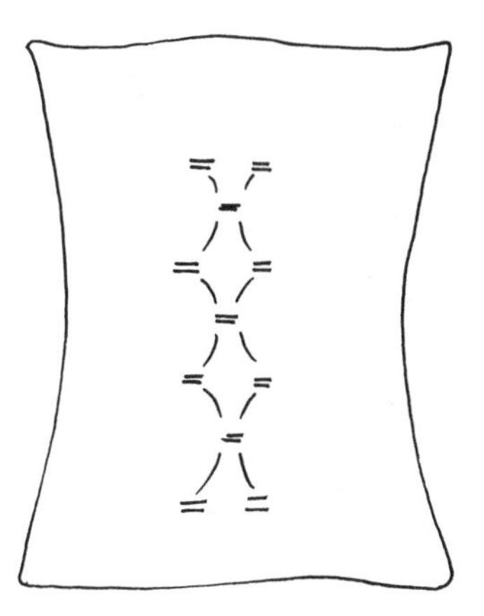

**Making the cushion back**

**6** Cut two pieces of fabric for the back, measuring 32 x 28cm (12½ x 11in), plus 1.5cm (½in) seam allowance. Fold over and stitch a neat 2cm (¾in) double hem on one long side of each piece of fabric.

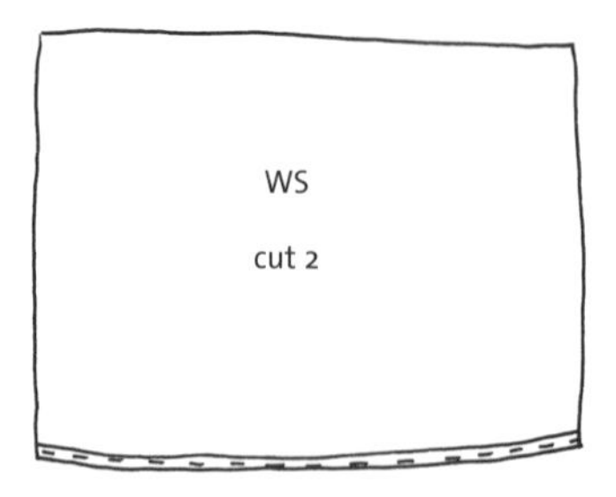


**7** Lay the smocked cushion front on a flat surface wrong side down. Take the two back pieces and place on top of each other right sides facing down, positioned so that the hemmed edges are towards the centre and overlap. Pin and machine stitch through all layers, with a 1.5cm (½in) seam allowance all around.

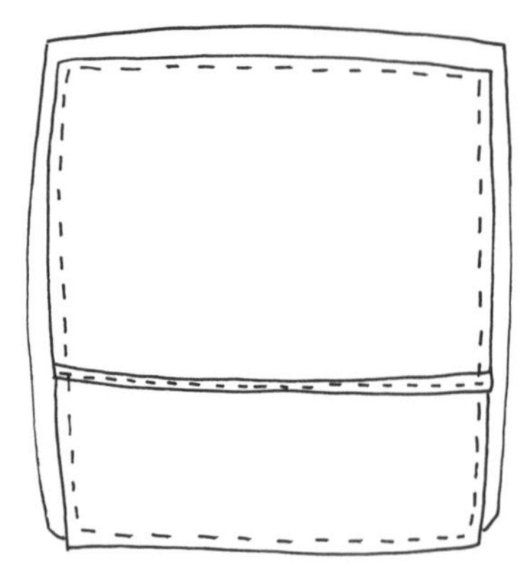

**8** Turn right sides out and insert your piece of wadding through the back vent.

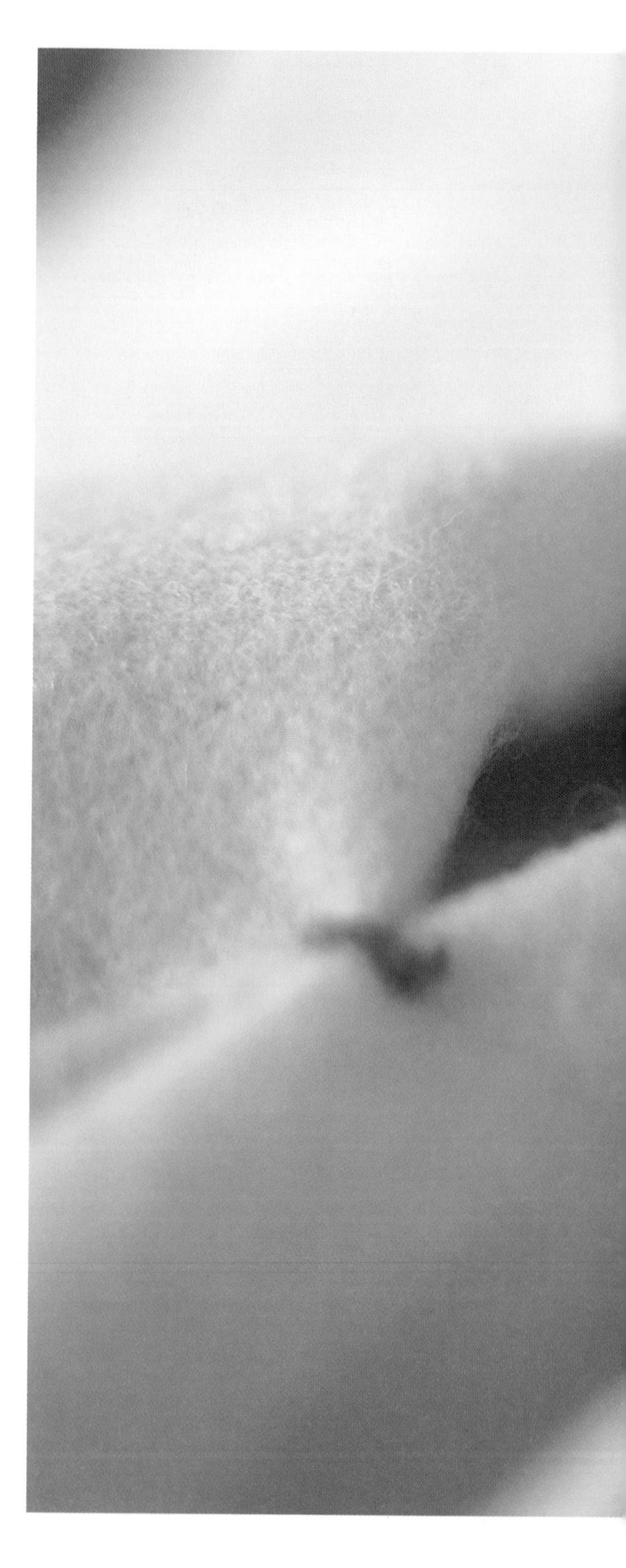

# apron

This apron, made with a combination of printed cotton and silk dupion for ties and the smocked pocket trim, ties around the waist. The ties are part of the extended waistband. The apron front measures 56cm (22in) long by 68cm (27in) wide.

### What you need

1m (1yd) piece of printed cotton fabric; 0.5m (½yd) piece of silk dupion; fabric-marking pencil; six-stranded cotton thread; sewing needle.

### Cutting out the fabrics

**1** Cut a piece of printed fabric for the main part of the apron measuring 52 x 62cm (20½ x 24½in), plus 1.5cm (½in) seam allowance.

Cut a piece of silk dupion measuring 84 x 6cm (33 x 2¼in) to form the smocked pocket top, plus 1.5cm (½in) seam allowance.

Cut a piece of printed cotton measuring 30cm (12in) square, plus 1.5cm (½in) seam allowance, to form the apron pocket.

Cut a piece of fabric measuring 1.8m x 7cm (2yd x 2¾in) in each of the silk dupion and printed cotton for the waistband/ties, plus 1.5cm (½in) seam allowance.

### Making the smocked pocket trim

**2** Mark out a 2.5cm (1in) square grid on the reverse side of the dupion fabric with 17 folds and 5 stitch marks (see page 118).

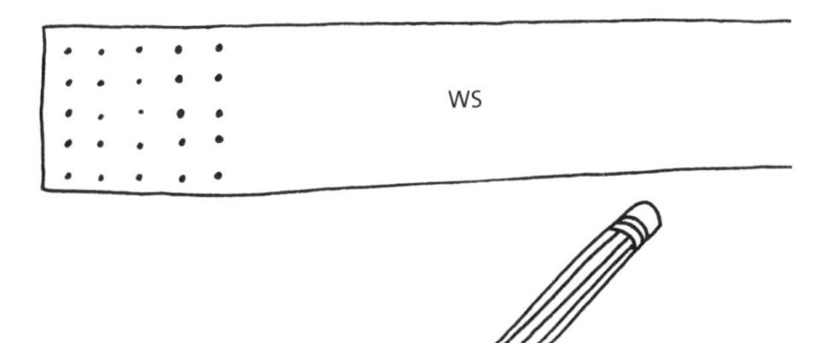


**3** Gather the fabric with running stitches (see page 118) and then turn to the right side and smock into a diamond pattern using matching thread (see page 119).

**4** Stitch a 1.5cm (½in) hem on the sides and top of the smocked trim. Place the smocked trim on the top of the pocket fabric, curving it slightly. Mark the shape of the lower edge of the smocked trim on the pocket with a fabric-marking pencil. Cut away the pocket fabric along the marked line.

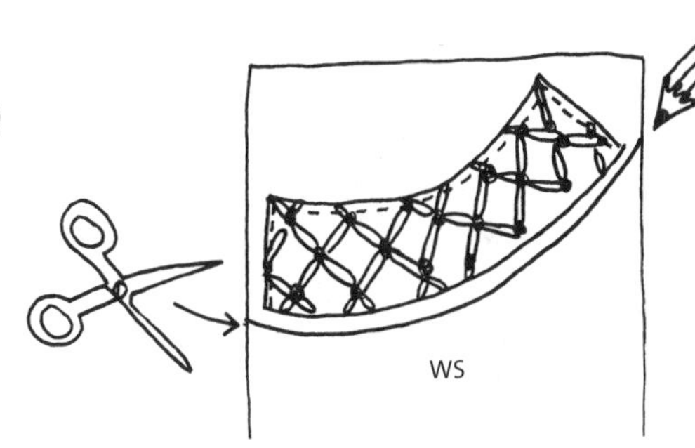


**5** Flip the pocket trim and place on the pocket fabric, right sides facing. Pin and sew along the curved stitching line. Press open the seam so that the fabric lies flat, and clip the seam allowance if necessary to maintain a flat curve.

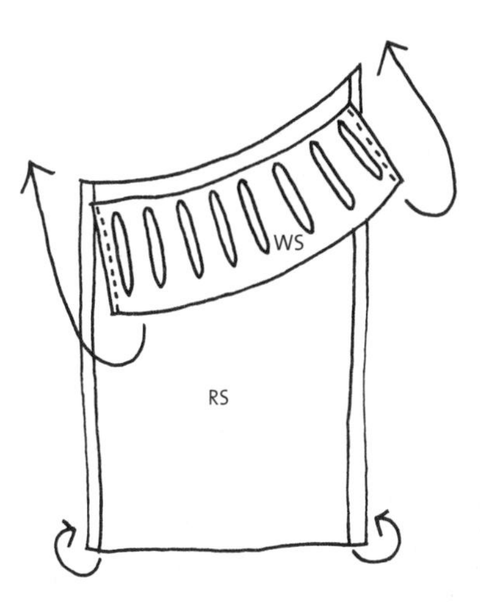

**6** Fold under the two sides of the pocket by 1.5cm (½in) to the wrong side. Pin and press flat. Place the pocket wrong side down on the right side of the main apron fabric, matching corners. Topstitch the two sides of the pocket. Fold under the apron hem and sides, and topstitch.

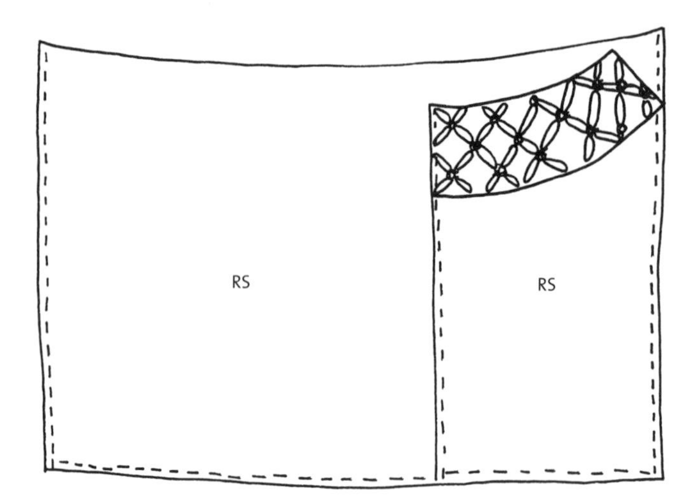


**Making the waistband and ties**

**7** Place a strip of silk dupion and printed cotton right sides together. Taking a 1.5cm (½in) seam allowance, machine stitch the sides and one long edge. Clip the corners and press open the seams. Turn right sides out and press flat. Fold the raw edge under by 1.5cm (½in).

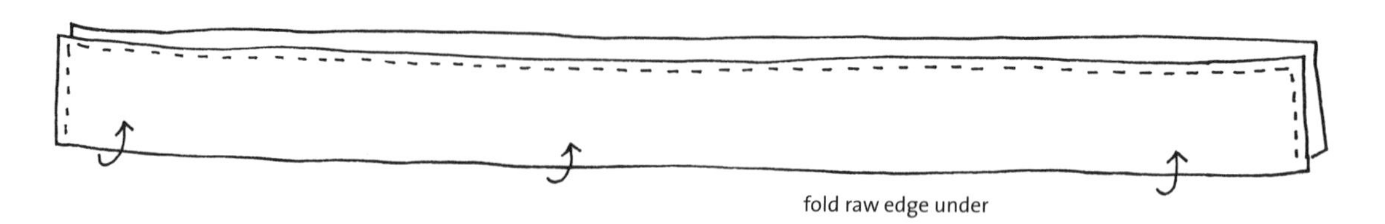


**8** Mark the centres of the apron and the waistband with pins. Slip the top edge of the apron into the opening of the waistband/tie, matching the centre points. Topstitch the waistband/tie in place to attach it to the apron body.

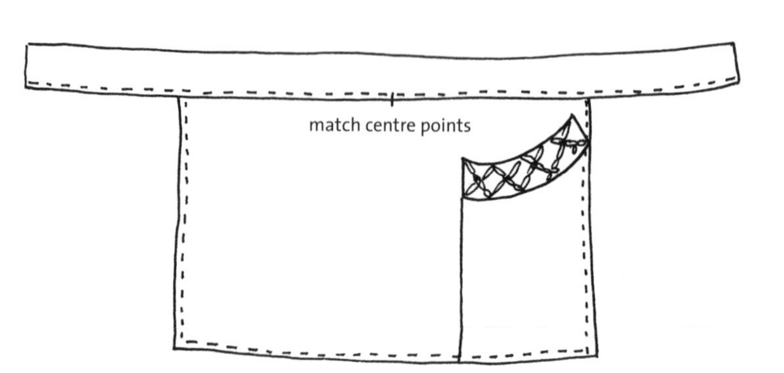

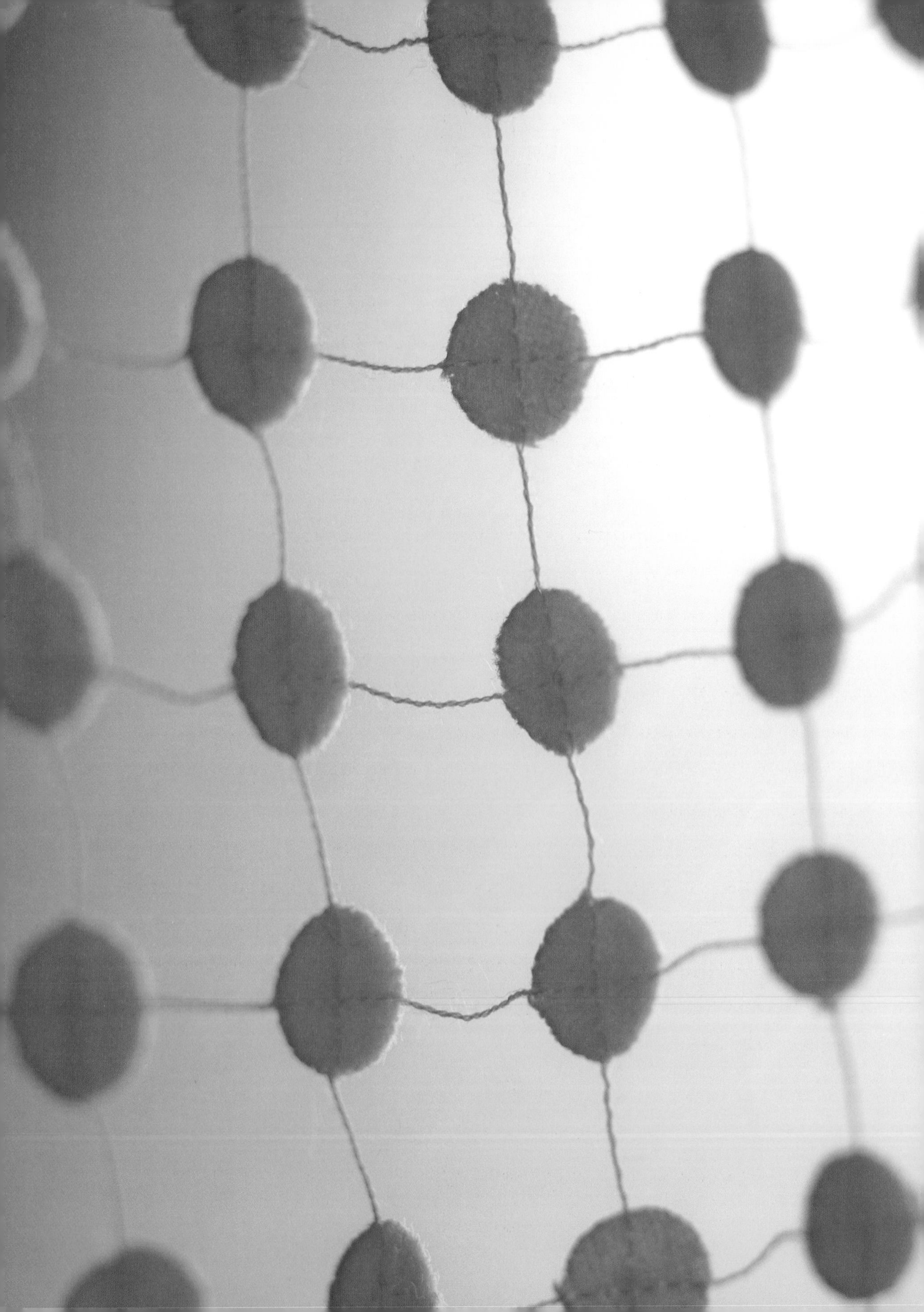

# special fabrics

● ● ● ● ● ● ● ● ● ● ● ●

The techniques in this chapter are a little different, as the fabrics are used in a very particular way – to allow you to stitch without always having the structure of a standard base fabric. Instead they are worked with two types of temporary base (stabilizing) fabrics; Stitch 'n' Tear and a dissolvable fabric, Aquafilm.

Stitch 'n' Tear provides a backing for weaker, lightweight fabrics that might distort when stitched. It is primarily a stabilizer. It is a non-woven fabric, similar in appearance to interfacing. If the Stitch 'n' Tear fabric is placed on the back of the fabric being stitched it prevents the fabric from pulling. Afterwards the Stitch 'n' Tear fabric is torn away.

Aquafilm is a thick, transparent plastic fabric that can take the strain of heavy-duty stitching. It is made from a seaweed base and will dissolve in warm water, so after washing only the stitching remains. The joy of this dissolvable fabric is that it allows you free rein to create some very lacy, delicate textiles of your own design. You can even incorporate items like feathers, bits of other fabrics, or whatever you fancy into the final piece. In this, it is quite unlike anything else you might come across.

Your stitching creates the fabric and this technique lends itself to free-embroidery. When stitching free-embroidery, lower the teeth (the feed dogs) on the sewing machine so they cease to grip the fabric. To compensate, you stitch with the fabric held in a hoop, so that you are using the sewing machine rather like a drawing tool. There is also a special free-embroidery foot that can be attached to the sewing machine that prevents the fabric accidentally getting gripped by the needle.

◀ I used dissolvable fabric to create this fabric, in which the discs are held together by gossamer-like threads.

## design samples

These samples show how to use the two different kinds of temporary base fabrics to create effects where the stitching is the primary element of the fabric. The result is airy, lighter-weight fabrics that are particularly good for edgings or trims, like those on the throw on page 134. Among the many projects you can create using these fabrics are lace-like edgings and insertions for throws, mats or blinds, for example, or for garments, as well as larger pieces of translucent fabric that can be made into screens of various kinds.

Your choice of fabrics and threads requires careful consideration, to ensure that they hold together once the temporary base fabric is removed. You can make monochromatic stitched textiles, like an organic form of randomly stitched lace, or you can layer small strips or pieces of fabric on top of each other and join them with a contrasting thread colour.

The important point to bear in mind is that once the temporary base fabric has been removed, only the stitches you have made hold the new fabric together, so make sure the stitched lines connect with the remaining fabric or each other to create a supporting structure.

You can work with fine or thick threads, depending on the style of the design. The samples here all use straight stitch, but you can use more intricate stitches, too.

A

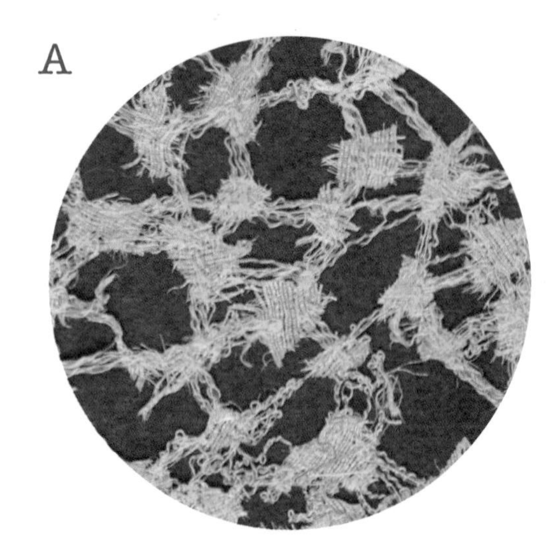

▲ **Sample A:** This sample was made by laying small pieces of silk between two sheets of Aquafilm. Random stitching was applied all over the surface of the pieces to ensure that they were linked, before the Aquafilm was washed way. The resulting lace has been stitched to a dark base fabric.

B

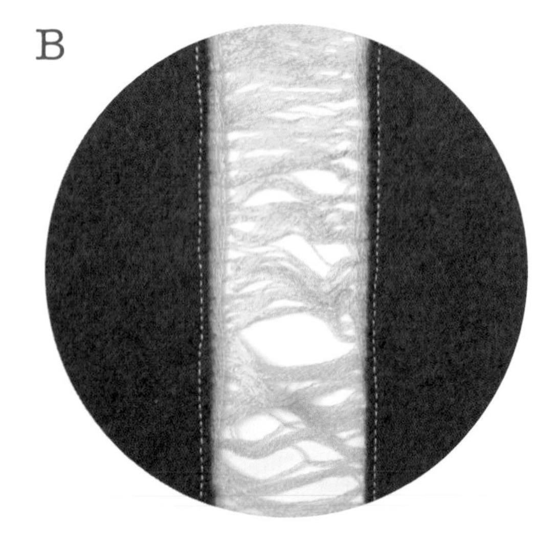

▲ **Sample B:** Here, the delicately stitched insertion was made using a standard sewing thread machine stitched onto Aquafilm. Once the dissolvable fabric was washed away, the insertion was machine stitched between two pieces of wool, using a straight stitch in contrasting thread.

C

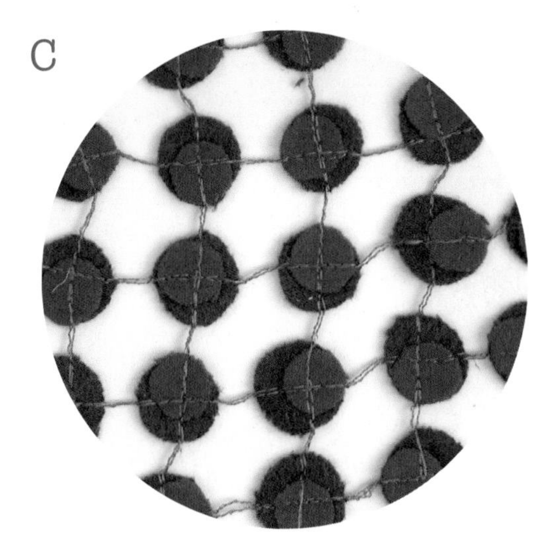

▲ **Sample C:** For this sample, pairs of red and grey wool circles were placed in a grid formation, sandwiched between two layers of Aquafilm, and stitched together. When the dissolvable fabric was washed away, the circles remained linked.

E

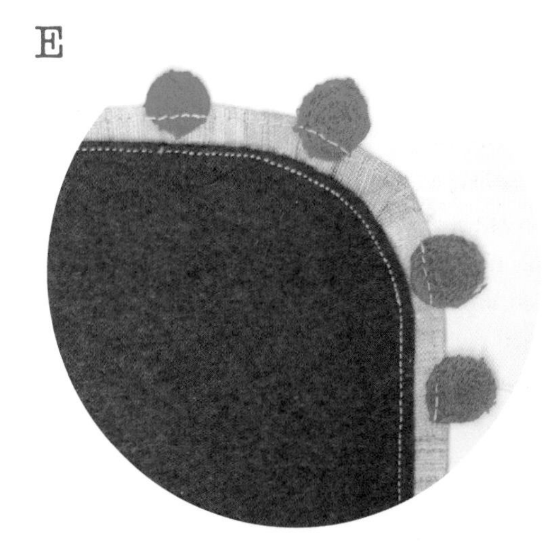

▲ **Sample E:** These red circles were created individually by stitching around in a circular motion on Aquafilm. They were then topstitched along the edge of a piece of bias-cut fabric as a trim.

D

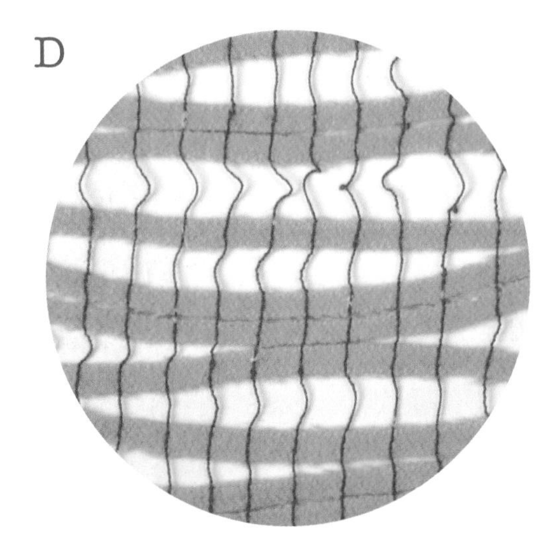

▲ **Sample D:** Here, strips of yellow woollen fabric were laid in narrowly spaced horizontal rows between two layers of Aquafilm. They were then stitched vertically using red cotton thread; the fabric remained connected in loose rows once the Aquafilm was dissolved.

F

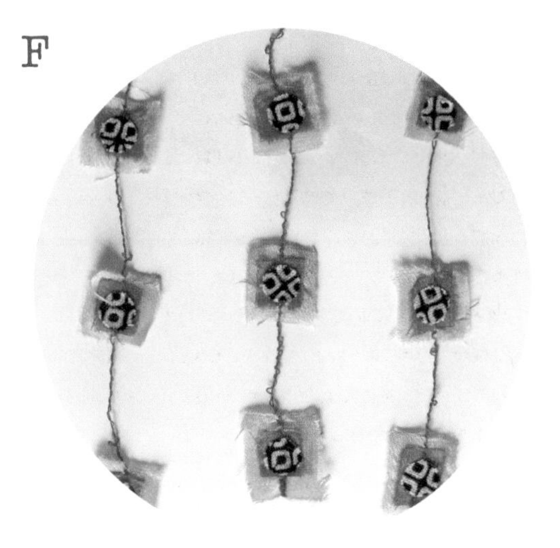

▲ **Sample F:** Here, a delicate fringing has been created by stitching small layered pieces of fabric together with red thread onto Stitch 'n' Tear beyond the edge of the base fabric.

# how to use special fabrics

An embroidery hoop is required when stitching with both Stitch 'n' Tear and Aquafilm to hold the work in place (**1a**).

**Using a hoop**

To prepare your fabric and hoop for use, loosen the tension screw on the outer hoop, then place the outer hoop on your work surface and put your fabric over it. Now place the inner hoop over the top of the fabric and push the inner hoop down into the outer hoop (**1b**). Tighten the tension screw. Gently pull on the fabric around the outside of the hoops to make it taut inside the hoop. Keep on pulling the fabric gently while continuing to tighten the screw. Work slowly and gently, pulling the fabric in opposing directions on all sides (**1c**). The fabric should be drum taut.

To stitch free-embroidery using the hoop, use a free-embroidery foot, drop the feed dogs on the machine feed and guide the hoop in the direction you want to stitch (**1d**). If your embroidery is large, you may need to unscrew and reposition the hoop to complete the design.

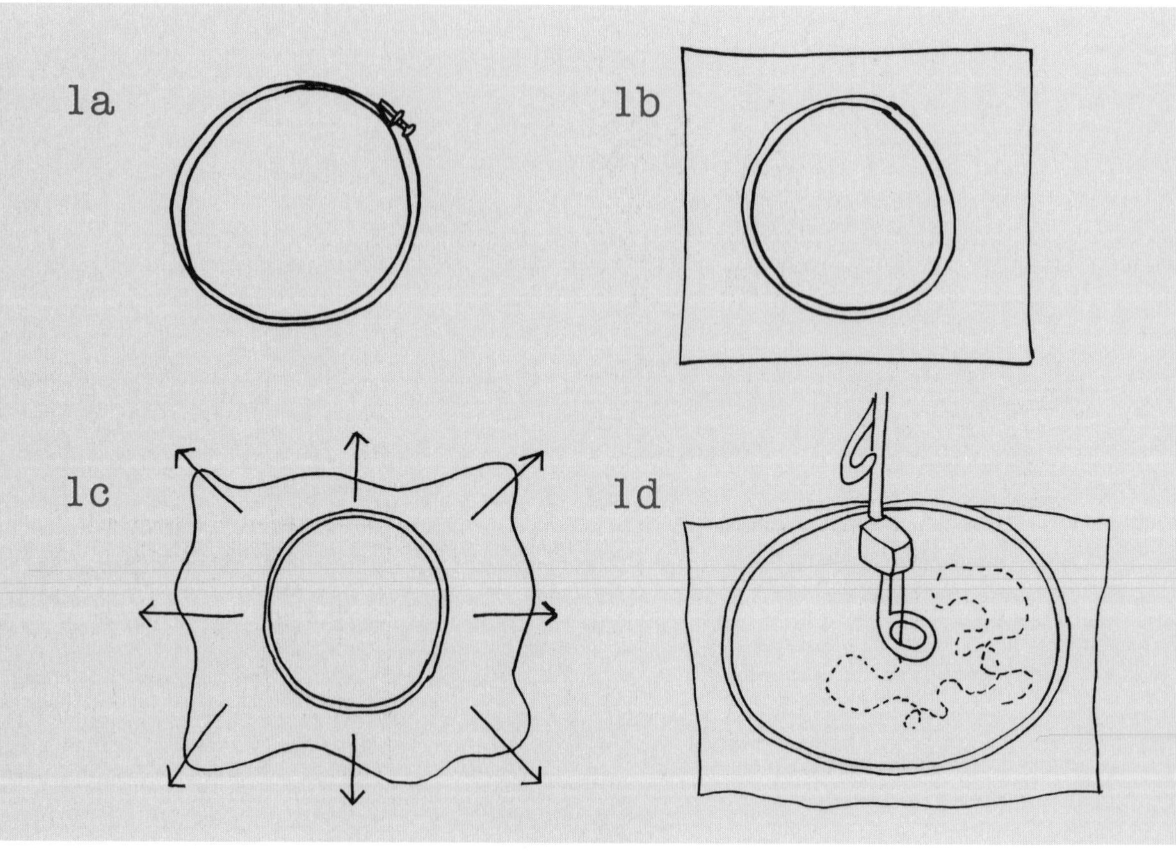

### Using Aquafilm

Before using Aquafilm, always make sure your fabric and thread are colourfast. Put the Aquafilm in an embroidery hoop (see above). Stitch your design (by hand or machine) and when complete remove your work from the hoop. Cut off any excess Aquafilm around the edges (**2**). Fill a basin or sink with warm water. Put your stitched fabric into the water, keeping it flat. Gently agitate the work and, using your fingers and thumbs, carefully work the Aquafilm so that it starts to dissolve. To remove all traces of Aquafilm, keep refreshing the water, repeating the process and rinsing as required. You may need to do this several times to ensure that you have washed out all of the Aquafilm.

Lay your work on a flat surface, or cork pinboard, with a piece of plain fabric beneath. Pin it out and leave to dry. Remove the pins and backing fabric.

If your project is larger than an embroidery hoop, keep working in small sections of Aquafilm, then stitch the pieces together when dissolved.

### Using Stitch 'n' Tear

Cut a piece of Stitch 'n' Tear large enough to cover the size of the sample you are working on, or the area that needs stabilizing. If you are not working with an embroidery hoop, then tack your fabric onto a suitably sized piece of Stitch 'n' Tear fabric (**3**). Do the same even if you are only working within a small area of your sample. Complete the stitched design, then remove your work from the embroidery hoop, remove any tacking stitches and carefully tear away the Stitch 'n' Tear fabric from the stitched design (**4**).

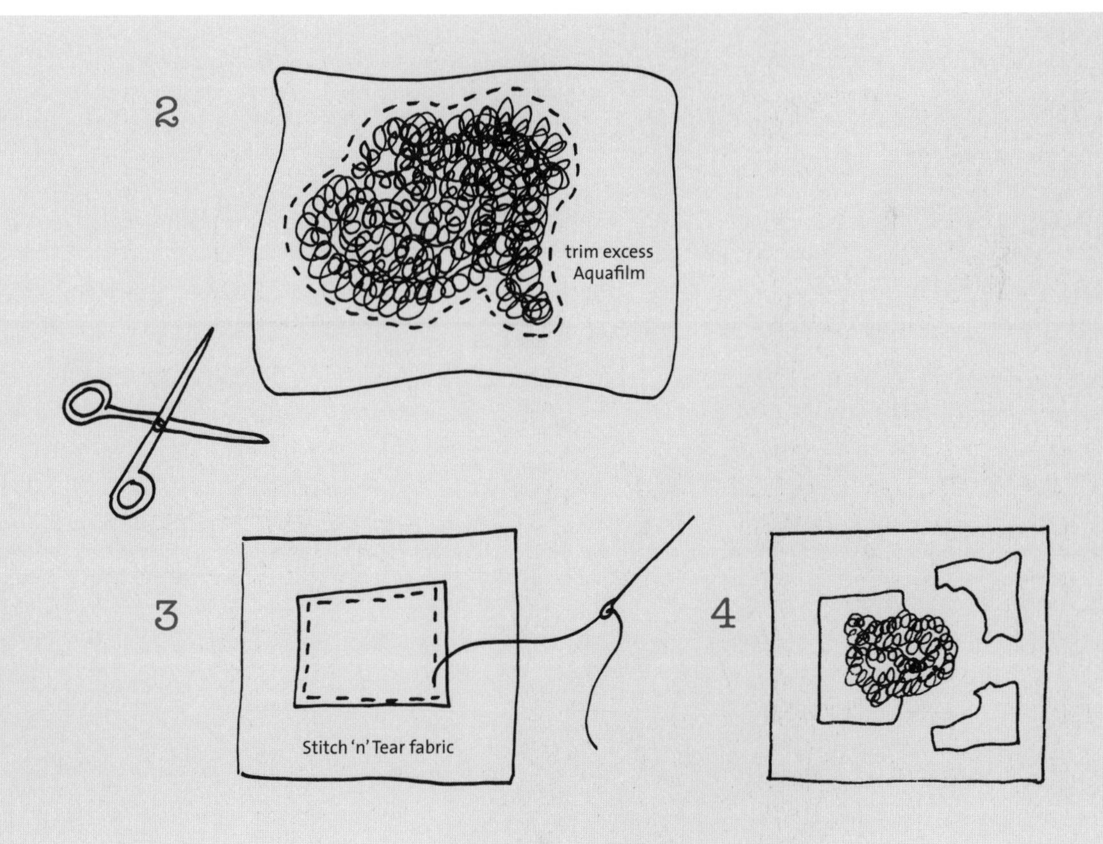

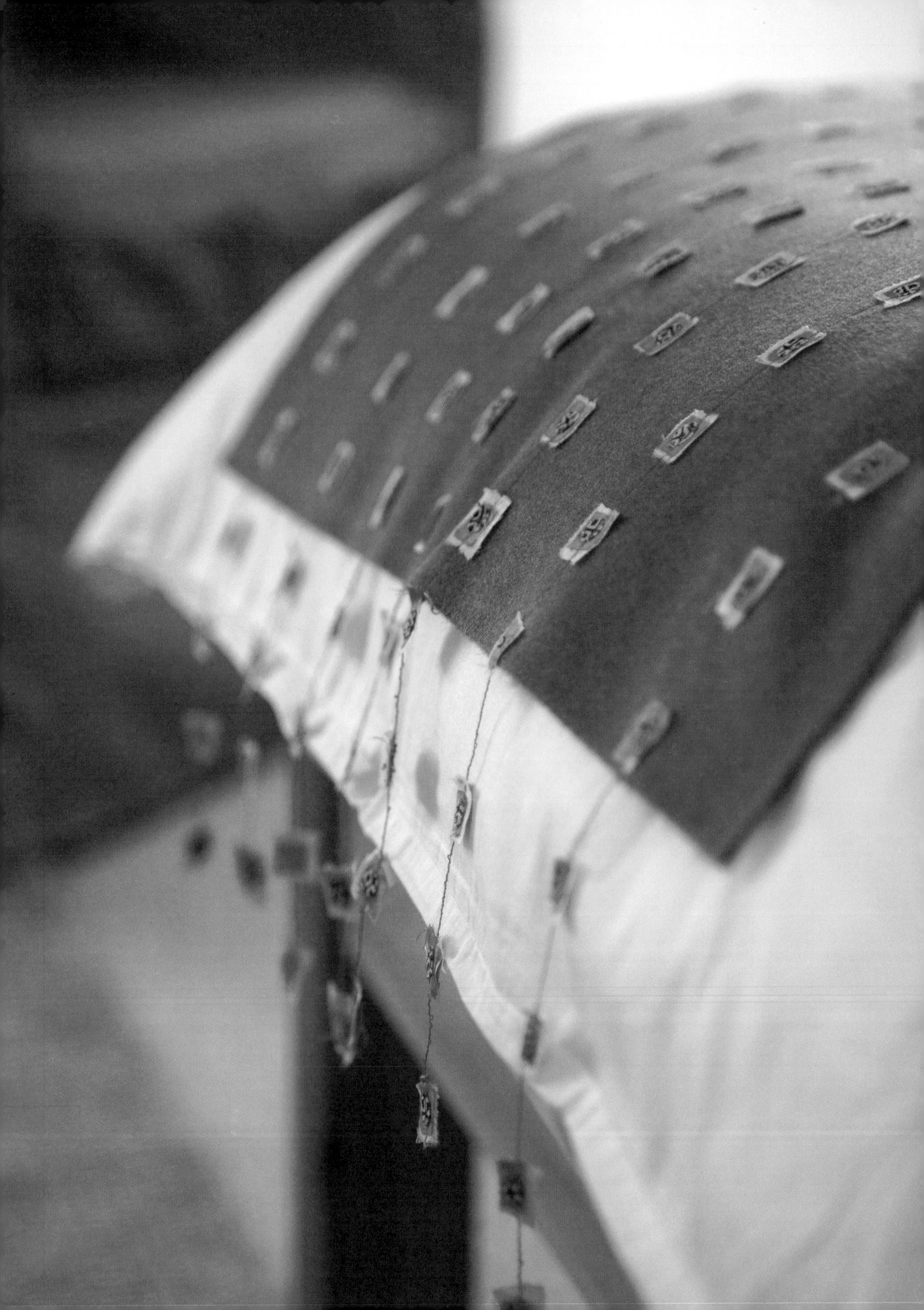

# fringed throw

This narrow, fringed throw has lines of appliqué shapes, stitched in rows, that turn into fringing at each end, created using Stitch 'n' Tear. The length of the decorative edging can vary to suit your project. The felt base does not fray so requires no hemming. This throw measures 147 x 61cm (58 x 24in).

**What you need**

Piece of woollen felt cut to size required; small amount each of silk in two contrasting colours; patterned fabric in toning colour; Stitch 'n' Tear fabric; revolving hole punch; ruler; tailor's chalk; fabric glue (optional); contrasting sewing thread.

**1** Cut two pieces of Stitch 'n' Tear each to the width of the throw and length of fringing. Pin one piece at each end of the woollen fabric. Using the ruler and tailor's chalk, mark out the stitching lines along the length of the fabric, and over the Stitch 'n' Tear, approximately 7.5cm (3in) apart.

**2** Tear one colour of the silk fabric into strips measuring 2cm (¾in) wide. Tear the other silk fabric into smaller 1.5cm (½in) wide strips.

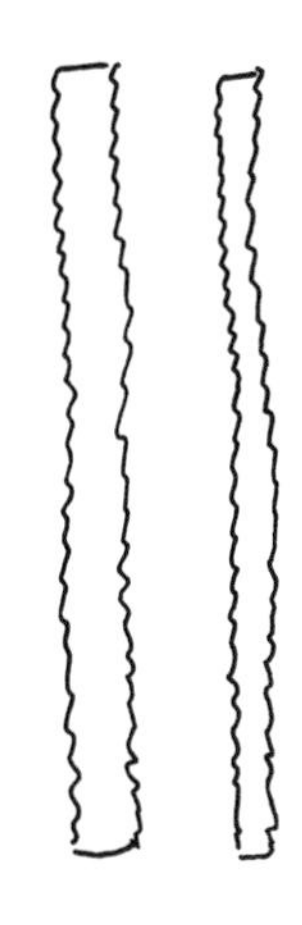

**3** Press these strips flat and cut each strip into squares with sharp embroidery scissors. Using a revolving hole punch, cut out some tiny 5mm (¼in) circles in the patterned fabric.

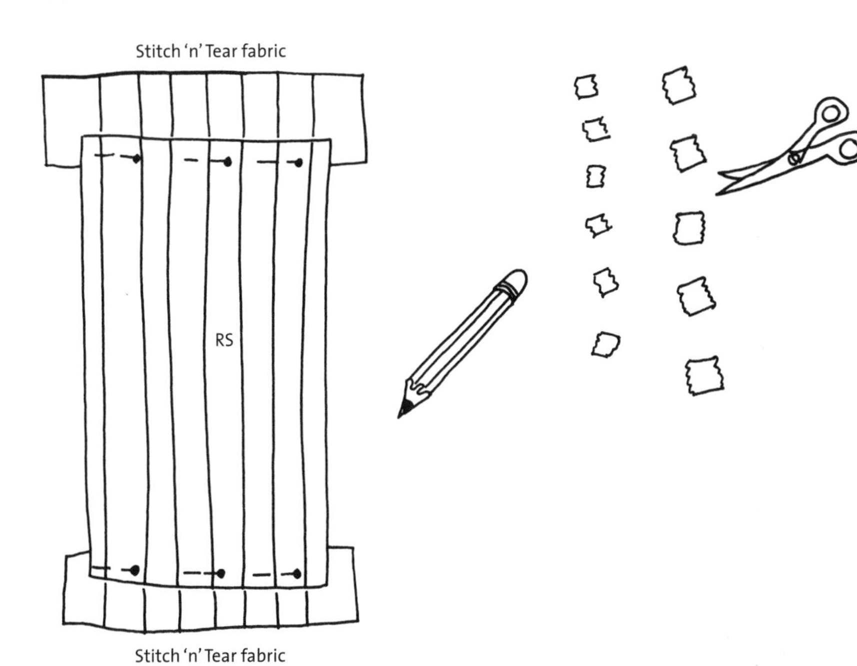

**4** Place a small square on top of a larger square and top with a circle. Either glue or hand stitch the layers with a cross stitch before you sew. If you don't do either, they will slip around.

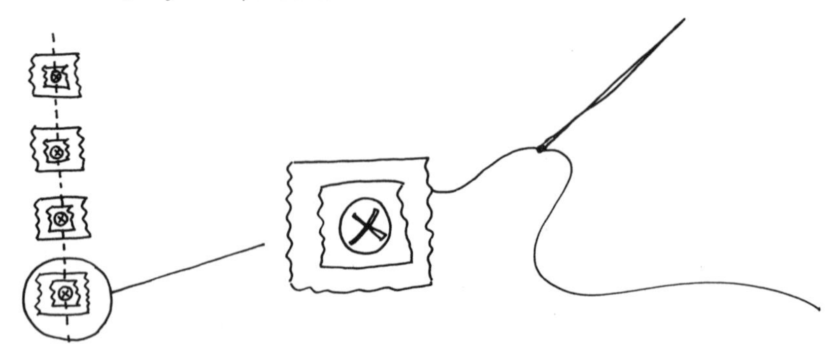

**5** Machine stitch the squares in place following your chalk lines as a guide. The fabric pieces can be placed randomly along the chalk line. On the Stitch 'n' Tear fabric, make sure you layer the circles and squares as follows: circle, small square, large square, small square, circle. This is because when you remove the Stitch 'n' Tear you will be able to see both sides of the little square pieces.

**6** When all the stitching is complete, very carefully tear away the Stitch 'n' Tear. Press the throw and fringe.

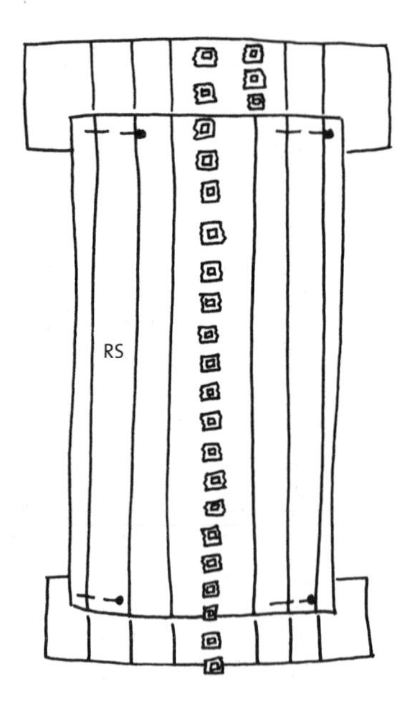


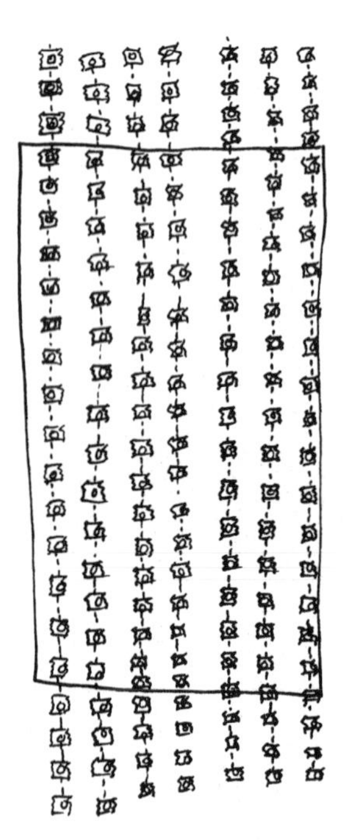

# lace-edged mat

This little mat made from woollen felt is finished with an organic, unstructured lace made using Aquafilm. The lacy fabric is cut into strips and applied to the mat as an edging. This mat measures 45 x 30cm (18 x 12in), including the edging.

**What you need**

0.25m (¼yd) woollen fabric for base; small amount of silk tussah for the lace; matching thread; piece of Aquafilm (twice size of mat); embroidery hoop; cork pinboard.

**Making the lace**

**1** Cut a piece of woollen felt measuring 40 x 25cm (16 x 10in). Cut out two pieces of Aquafilm, each measuring 36 x 25cm (14 x 10in).

**2** Randomly chop the silk tussah into small pieces, roughly 1.5cm (½in) square. Evenly distribute these on top of one piece of Aquafilm.

**3** Carefully place the second layer of Aquafilm on top of the first to encase the bits of fabric. Sew a straight stitch around the edge to ensure the pieces don't fall out.

**4** Place the prepared Aquafilm in an embroidery hoop. Set the sewing machine for free embroidery (see page 132) and, using a straight stitch, begin to sew straight lines to link up all the pieces of fabric. Stitch each line seven or eight times to ensure that it will hold and check that all the pieces of silk are connected so that the stitching and fabric will hold together when the Aquafilm base is dissolved.

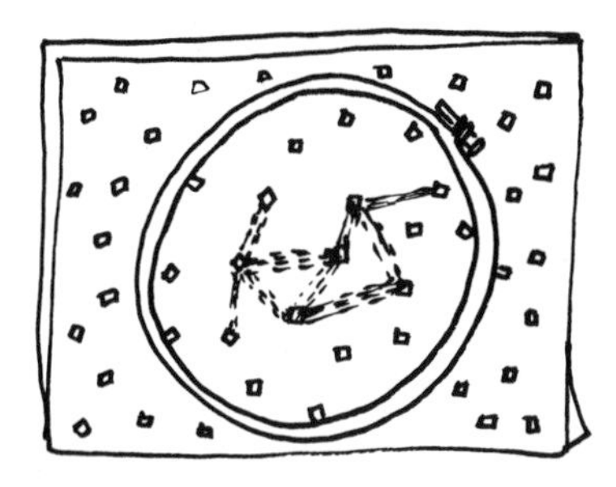

**5** Carefully wash away the Aquafilm and rinse until the fabric is clear (see page 133).

**6** Use a cork pinboard to pin out your fabric, so that it retains its original shape after it has been washed. Leave the fabric to dry.

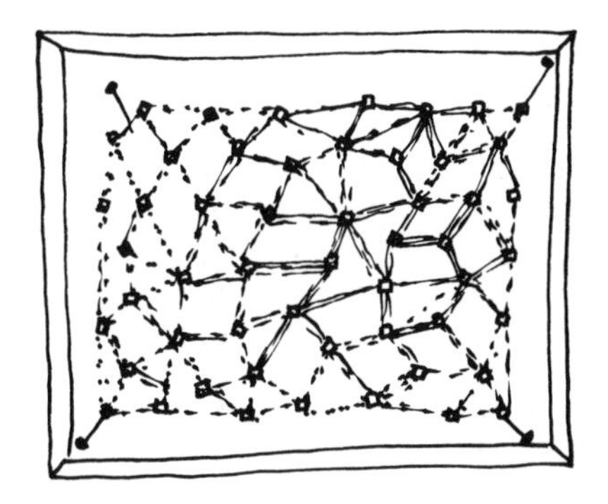

**7** Once dry, cut the fabric into four strips of equal width, approximately 6cm (2½in) wide, and position them around the edge of the woollen fabric. Pin into place and using a straight stitch, machine stitch to the woollen fabric. Hand stitch overlapping corners. Snip away any stray bits of fabric. Press the final piece.

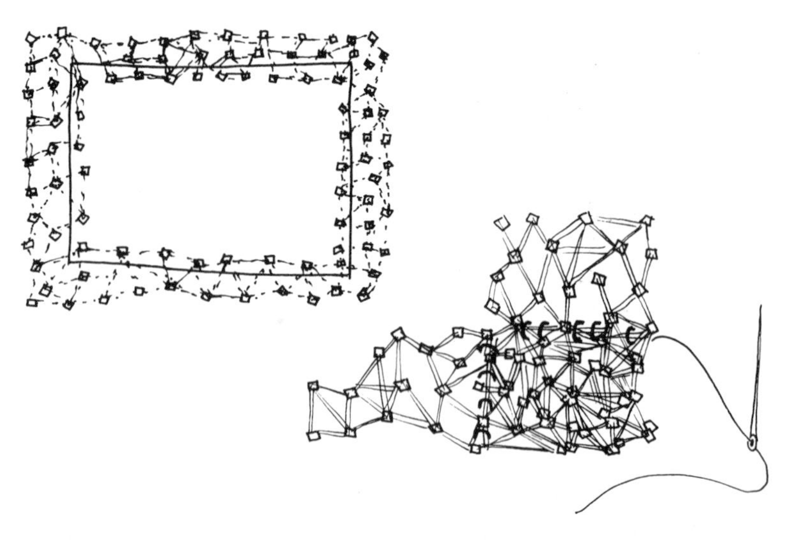

# useful information

I generally prefer to avoid too much measuring and marking when I am making stitched projects, so many of my designs are worked by simply positioning any decoration on the fabric by eye. I also quite like the slight wonkiness that occurs when the rows are not absolutely straight or consistently spaced, or if any little elements within the rows are not identical. However, this is not an excuse for being slapdash with the actual construction. The cutting out needs to be exact and the stitching done neatly and carefully.

A good way to avoid mark-making on fabric is to choose printed fabrics for your designs. Those with geometric patterns, like stripes and checks, provide a natural guide for lines of machining, for example.

**Finding inexpensive fabrics**

When sourcing fabrics remember you don't necessarily have to buy new. Vintage shops and fairs, and charity shops, are always good for interesting finds. Dresses and skirts can be recycled and old curtains reinvented as amazing cushions. It also pays to look out for unusual accessories, such as buckles and buttons. You may well have vintage finds hidden away in your loft or wardrobe.

You may need to repair small holes in vintage fabrics. Simply cut a piece from the edge of the fabric, just a little larger in circumference than the hole you want to patch. Fold over the raw edges, press, and pin the patch in place on top of the hole, matching any pattern. Stitch neatly and carefully around the edges with matching thread. Press so that the patch lies flat.

Inevitably, you will make a few mistakes. If you cut a piece of fabric too small, think about joining it to another piece and hiding the join with some form of decoration or cut up other pieces and make a patchwork design. Press seams after sewing to ensure the fabric sits flat. Keep any mistakes, as they can always be used at some point for smaller projects or for sampling.

**Caring for fabrics**

Take care of your fabrics by washing and pressing in the right way and always follow any cleaning instructions. When washing vintage fabrics, remember that pure wool should never be washed in a washing machine but it can be hand-washed in very cool water with special hand-washing soap flakes. Use a pressing cloth between the fabric and the iron when pressing delicate fabrics.

**Changing colours**

If you cannot find precisely the colour you want, consider creating your own colours. It is easy to dye natural fabrics, such as cottons and linens, in a washing machine. However, woollen fabric may shrink at the temperatures required for dyeing.

'Antique' plain, new white fabrics by tea-dyeing them so that they take on a softer hue. Make a very strong brew of tea, pour into a washing-up bowl, and dip in pre-dampened fabric. Agitate until the fabric has absorbed all the tea colour. Rinse out in clean water and hang up to dry.

**Turning your designs into gifts**

If you have gone to the trouble of making a design as a special gift for someone, then take care to finish and present it appropriately. You could make some pretty designer labels (try hand-stitching your name on narrow sewing tape) or decorate simple paper labels with a few hand stitches. To present your gift, such as one of the necklaces, wrap it in tissue paper and make a simple calico bag (a miniature version of the bag on page 108, perhaps), then attach a handmade label to the drawstring.

# suppliers

**Sources**

John Lewis
Oxford Street
London W1
08456 049 049
www.johnlewis.com
*Fabrics, haberdashery, yarns and threads*

The Cloth House
98 Berwick Street
London W1F 0QJ
00 44 (0) 20 7287 1555
www.clothhouse.com
*Great source of beautiful fabrics*

Ian Mankin
271/273 Wandsworth Bridge Road
London SW6 2TX
00 44 (0) 20 7722 0997
www.ianmankin.co.uk
*Renowned for natural furnishing fabrics*

Beyond Fabrics
67 Columbia Road
London E2 7RG
0044 (0) 20 7729 5449
www.beyond-fabrics.com
*Fabrics, haberdashery plus workshops and courses*

Habu textiles
135 West 29th Street, Suite 804
New York, NY 10001
00 212 239 3546
www.habutextiles.com
*Japanese yarns and fabrics*

www.misformake.co.uk
*Online seller of contemporary vintage-style prints*

VV Rouleaux
261 Pavilion Road
London SW1X 0PB
00 44 (0)20 7730 3125
www.vvrouleaux.com
*Beautiful ribbons and trimmings*

The Button Queen
76 Marylebone Lane
W1U 2PR
00 44 (0) 20 7935 1505
www.thebuttonqueen.co.uk
*Antique and contemporary buttons*

www.pfaffmachines.co.uk
*Suppliers of sewing machines*

www.coatscrafts.com
*Suppliers of haberdashery*

**Inspiration**

Fashion and Textile Museum
83 Bermondsey Street
London SE1 3XF
00 44 (0) 20 7407 8664
www.ftmlondon.org

Victoria & Albert Museum
Cromwell Road
London SW7 2RL
00 44 (0) 20 7942 2000
www.vam.ac.uk

**Blogs**

www.sewingfromthehill.typepad.com
www.selvedge.org/blog

# index

Projects are in **bold** type

# acknowledgements

I would like to thank Susan James at A & C Black, UK, and Melanie Falick at Stewart, Tabori & Chang, in New York, for giving me the opportunity to write and put this book together. Without their commitment this book would have remained a vision of mine. Many thanks to Susan Berry, who has been an absolute inspiration and guide to me. I cannot thank her enough for her continued support. Many thanks to John Heseltine, who always conjures the most amazing photographic shots, together with Susan's stunning ideas for styling. Also thanks to Anne Wilson, for producing such lovely layouts and to Katie Hardwicke, who is always spot on in the editorial department.

I would also like to thank my Mum and Dad, Pam and Clive, to whom this book is dedicated, for all of their help and encouragement. Finally, many thanks to my adorable nephews, Daniel and Matthew Breen, who constantly ask me to make things with them! While writing this book our making sessions have had to take a backseat, so we have lots of creativity to catch up on!